The Male Homemaker's Handbook

or

Never Kiss A Kid
Who's Just Eaten A Toad

by

Tom Pinnock

Pinnock, Tom
The Male Homemaker's Handbook: Or Never Kiss a Kid Who's Just
Eaten A Toad

ISBN # 1-882467-15-9

Library of Congress Catalog Card # 96-61715

Cover Design: Davison and Associates
Cover Art: © Mark S. Raithel 1996

Also available on audio cassette
To order Wildstone books and cassettes call toll free:
(800) 296-1918

Wildstone Media
401 Bussen Underground Rd.
St. Louis, MO 63129
(314) 487-0402

Introduction

I am fully aware that in many parts of the country the sexual lines in the division of labor are disappearing rapidly, and in a perfect world what is being said in this book would be an anachronism. But this is not a perfect world, and enlightenment is not as easy as stepping out of a cave and into the sun.

Changes in thinking do not occur en masse as many would wish or as some magazines might lead you to believe. Edification comes one person at a time. Consequently, in the following pages what I have done is to describe my journey out of an intellectual cave in which I not only found sunshine but a whole new way of looking at things.

However, it wasn't accomplished without bumping into stuff. Consequently, *The Male Homemaker's Handbook* is meant as a laugh-filled challenge to those who still regard sexual equality as just a concept. I freely admit that at the time the things in this book were occurring, they weren't always funny to me. But when I started laughing, too, I knew I had finally made it into a brave new world.

One filled with grins.

Dedication

"The Male Homemaker's Handbook *or* Never Kiss a Kid Who's Just Eaten a Toad" is dedicated to the two special women in my life — my wife, Karen, and my mom, Ann Pinnock. To me, they represent the millions of women around the world, who have the toughest and perhaps most important jobs on earth, being moms and homemakers.

Yes, this book is meant as a tribute to them and all the other fearless women who not only rear children, but find time to care for their husbands and provide the inspiration to keep communities decent places to live. From my perspective, their job is arduous, and one that's not only misunderstood but unappreciated by those of us who have never had to fill that role.

My beautiful bride, and the mother of our three children, has shown me that there is more to love than the passion of two hearts joined by an invisible thread. The sacrifice, energy and time that Karen has given our children is almost beyond my comprehension. Not only is she kind and caring, but she is supportive and helpful — with them and with me.

She knows the little things like where the kids' shoes are, who's spending the night with whom, which kid needs a bath and which kid won't eat macaroni. Watching her has given me insight into caring and generosity.

My mom reared seven children and then went on to become a successful businesswoman. She has always been a tireless, cheerful individual, who loved her family and stood beside her children no matter what troubles came their way.

Growing up, we didn't have much money, but there were countless gifts that she managed to provide, important things like enjoying life, maintaining a positive outlook and believing in ourselves and the good people around us. It wasn't until I was grown and had children of my own that I began to understand how much she loved me and my brothers and sisters.

To you, Karen and Mom, I want you and everyone else to know that I love you both very much.

So for you, and for all the other wonderful moms, these pages are given to you.

Acknowledgments

Of the people who stepped in and helped with this project, I first have to thank Dick Richmond,who saw the potential in what I had to offer when my manuscript was still in raw stages. Not only did he encourage me to complete the book, he worked with me every step of the way, making suggestions, editing and pulling everything together into an arrangement that flows.

In addition, I am most grateful for the critical eyes of Elaine Viets, Cleora Hughes and Paul Richmond, who gave their time and considerable talent to read over the manuscript and to point out areas that could be improved.

Chapter 1

Citrus Wars And A Skinny Blonde

B ack in the 1950s, probably there was no better place in the world for a child to grow up than Central Florida. The region just north of Orlando was filled with orange groves and forests of pine and oak spaced nicely by hundreds of lakes teeming with bass and alligators. The Dwight D. Eisenhower Interstate Highway System was still in the planning stages and Interstate 4 wasn't even a consideration. Instead, the little towns that I knew — Altamonte Springs, Longwood and Lake Mary — were criss-crossed by dirt roads that saw more action by cows and kids than by cars and trucks.

Change is inevitable, of course, but when Disney World opened its gates in 1972, it seemed as if every person on the planet came to town, and many of them stayed. Old highways were widened, new ones were built and tourists were everywhere except in the orange groves, because the trees had disappeared to make room for concrete. Within a blink it seemed, hotels, malls and subdivisions shot up on that concrete like magic.

But for many of us who lived there, it was black magic. Suddenly, it seemed we had to start locking our doors at night. A rough element moved in and with it drugs and crime. Instead of the stability I had understood as mine when I was a boy, the atmosphere became transient and familiar faces were replaced by a endless string of strangers.

You can't turn back the clock, but there are moments when I wish my children could know the same simple environment I enjoyed as a youngster. That was a time when neighbors knew one another, and sandlot baseball was the king of entertainment, and television was just a minor recreation.

You can't blame television for everything, but it wasn't as important when I was growing up. I spent much of my time in orange groves playing with the other kids. We'd divide up into teams and battle one another in what I fondly remember as our citrus wars. Our weapons were oranges, tangerines and the occasional grapefruit. When we got tired and sticky, we'd sit down and eat our ammunition.

In that gummy crowd was a skinny little blonde with a pretty face and a strong right arm. I don't remember when I started chasing her around the orange groves, but I know the exact hour when the chase ended. It was the morning of the day we got married 20 years after the pursuit commenced. By then, Karen Sims was beautiful, svelte and still kind of little. But woman-sized little.

By the time we made it to the altar, the fragrance of orange blossoms was almost history in our area. Orange trees will not stand in the way of progress and bulldozers. Neither can they resist Jack Frost on his occasional visits. In the late '80s, Jack got the rest of those wonderful trees when he came to stay for a few days a couple of years in a row.

But when Karen and I bought our first house, it was in Longwood and we had orange trees. There were only three of them and they weren't big, but they were ours.

I was thrilled. A few days after we moved in, however, my mother-in-law, Joyce Sims, came over toting a chainsaw to help out with the yardwork. Before I could say tangerine, she felled those trees and tossed them into the swamp behind our house.

My face must have expressed my horror, because as soon as she looked up, her smile of accomplishment vanished. Shrugging, she switched off the chainsaw, and said, apologetically, ''I had no idea you wanted to keep those sickly little trees.''

"That's OK," I answered bravely. Then I turned and watched in disbelief as the last three orange trees in the entire county drifted slowly into the darkness of the swamp.

In retrospect, that was only a minor glitch as Karen and I tried to build a life for ourselves. By the time we got enough money to make a down payment on that house, we had three children — Lindsay, Tommy and Ashley. Unfortunately, we didn't get to be with them as much as we wanted. Like so many American couples today, Karen and I both had to work in an attempt to make ends meet, she as a nurse, me as a newspaper reporter.

It was a struggle, and I was doing my best to believe that it was worth it. I kept saying to myself, "I've got a beautiful wife, three great kids and a mother-in-law who's a terror with a chainsaw. What more could a man want?"

But there was more — and for Karen, too. Deep in our hearts, we felt that one of us needed to stay home with the children. Funny thing was that both of us wanted to be the one who did it. What was even funnier is that I was the one who tried.

Chapter 2

From Deadlines to Diapers

L ooking back, I can't imagine why I thought that being a homemaker would be such a snap. In my working life, I've been a soldier, a firefighter and a newspaper reporter. Interesting jobs, but they sure didn't teach me how to be a mother, a cook and a maid. The only exception was my life as a firefighter, an experience that has proven to be very valuable in the kitchen.

I'm ashamed to admit this now, but there was a time when I thought that real men didn't wash clothes, dry dishes or change diapers. In my mind, such mundane chores were reserved for women, and should be completed quickly, with little fuss and above all quietly. After all, what could be hard about cleaning a room, feeding a kid, and having the rest of the day to watch talk television?

That's what I used to think, but now that I've experienced the life of a homemaker, I can tell you that the job is not only endless, it's thankless, requiring the patience of an ice fisherman and the endurance of a marathon runner. What's worse is that the pay is lousy.

My journey into the world of diapers and mops got its start when I shot my mouth off to Karen about how I should be the one to stay home with the kids. At the time, I was a reporter with the Orlando Sentinel, but I had an idea about a home-based business that would free me from the long hours I spent covering my various beats at the newspaper. At the Sentinel, I wrote stories about subjects ranging from felons to fishing.

Karen worked as a nurse, taking care of sick people in their homes. Her hours were more flexible than mine, so she usually picked up our three children. Lindsay, then 6 years old, was in first grade and the younger two, Tommy, 3, and Ashley, 1, were in daycare. By the time Karen got home, most often she had only a few minutes to spend with them before getting down to her most challenging chore — cooking.

Just for the record, I've always been a big supporter of Karen's culinary efforts. I would give her an ''A'' for effort, but considering the end results, and grading on a curve, her report card would still have to be signed by her parents. Take for example what happened the other day with Lindsay.

''Daddy, I can't chew Mommy's oatmeal,'' Lindsay said almost in tears. ''It's too hard.''

''That's OK, Princess,'' I told her. ''Just knock off a chunk and dip it in your milk for a few minutes. It'll soften up.''

But we met those little challenges as they emerged, and they couldn't be critical to our main effort, which was survival. So while Karen stayed busy with her nursing and homemaking, I had to deal with tough editors, who were constantly putting deadline pressure on me, trying to coax me into shooting for angles or angling for fish, depending on the beat I happened to be assigned for the day.

''Pinnock, we need your fishing column by Friday,'' Mike Ludden would say as he wolfed down a cheese log. ''You'd better get out there and catch something.''

Some guys are just naturally good at fishing. Maybe, it's instinct; I don't know for sure. All I knew was that catching fish was a gift I didn't have. I didn't mind writing the column. I liked the lake life and being around fishermen. It was just that I always felt the fraud for appearing to be an expert about something I couldn't really do myself.

So I would fall into a funk, agonizing about where to hook a lunker, and eventually slip into one of those blame patterns in which you seek out someone else on which you can pin your failures. "Here, I am struggling," I would think, "and all Karen has to worry about is what she was going to cook for supper. She's got it made."

I was smart enough to keep those kinds of thoughts to myself, however, especially after the time I made a comparison regarding our different lifestyles. Up to that point, I never knew what quick hands Karen had. Faster than I could see it, she reached out and yanked down my lower lip. Considering it later, I realized my timing had been bad. When I mentioned it, she was in the process of throwing out a piece of meat she had just transformed into charcoal.

As for my journalism career, my bride had her own opinion about the value of what I was doing to earn a living. On more than one occasion, she mentioned that getting paid to reel in bass was the sham job of all time.

"That's a slap in the face," I protested. "Writing a fishing column is a grueling chore that requires considerable dedication, endurance and sacrifice."

Regarding me as if I had just acquired fins, she quipped, "Like getting out of bed when the sun is straight up."

"Pulling yourself out of the sack in the wee hours of the morning is tough," I countered defensively.

"Wee hours!" she sputtered, putting her hand on one of her little hips and glaring at the ceiling as if she might will something to fall on my head.

"Sure," I said, reminding her of the time that I made it to the bathroom before noon.

"Noon is not the wee hours."

"Well," I said, "for a reporter on a morning newspaper, that's the crack of dawn."

As I continued to grumble about the inhumanity of my situation, Karen splashed cold water into my face, saying "You're right. You can't let your readers down. Both would be so disappointed, especially your mother."

"I've got plenty of readers," I gurgled, toothpaste dribbling out of my mouth and onto my chin.

"And who knows," she said, ignoring my protests. "This time, you might even catch a fish."

"I've caught fish!" I yelled after her as she retreated into the next room.

Ironically, it was after a day of trying to catch one just to prove my point that I got into the business of folding the laundry and going to Brownie meetings. The sequence of events that led to this happened as I dragged myself into the house after work, and discovered smoke pouring from the kitchen.

"Are you in there?" I hollered to Karen. When she squealed in reply, I rushed in to see if I could save supper. "Think we oughta call the fire department?" I asked when I found her squirting Windex at the inferno that was making passes at her from the oven.

"They won't come," she wailed. "I've called them so many times, they said it would be in the family's best interest if the kitchen was destroyed."

I would have laughed but by then flames were licking up through the back burners and it was getting pretty warm. Well, actually, I did laugh later when Karen couldn't see me. But right then, I was busy snatching up what I thought was a canister of flour and heaving it onto the blaze. Unfortunately, I grabbed the sugar by mistake, and before I could recover, it quickly melted over the stove and onto the floor, making the kitchen look like a melt-down at a candy factory.

When the fire was finally Windexed into submission, I opened the oven and used a shovel to knock out the remains of dinner. Whatever it was, it bounced when it hit the floor and landed on my foot.

"It's like rubber," I said quietly, trying to shake the hot glob from the top of my shoe.

"That's because it is," Karen said. "I was trying to dry out Lindsay's sneakers."

I would have thrown up my hands in despair if I hadn't inadvertently glued one of them to the glob trying to pull it from my shoe. Then, too, the curious from next door and across the street had arrived, thinking perhaps that this time we had developed a real crisis.

Once the house was cleared of smoke and grinning neighbors, I started in on Karen.

"There's no supper on the table, the house is a mess and the kids are covered with soot. Do you have any idea what it's like to have to fish all day and then come home to this?"

Karen regarded me calmly, then casually flipped Lindsay's sneaker into the garbage. When she turned to face me, she folded her arms across her chest.

"We've talked about this before," she said, her blue eyes narrowing. "You always seem to forget that I work, too. At a real job."

"Real job...," I started to protest, and would have, too, if she hadn't backed me into a corner and pressed the forefinger of her throwing arm over my lips.

"One of us needs to stay home," she went on, "and since you seem to think being a homemaker is such a piece of cake..."

Breaking my lips loose for a moment, I challenged her with, "when's the last time we had cake in this house?

"...and since you can't catch a fish anyway," she continued, ignoring my quip and putting another lip lock on me, "And because you have some crazy notion that you can run your own little business off the kitchen table, well, I think you should do it.

My anger melted faster than Lindsay's sneaker, and I tried to grin. "Of course," she said, removing that lethal digit from under my nose, "I don't think you'll do very well."

With that, my anger flared again brighter than our recent fire. "You mean to tell me that you don't consider me capable of taking care of the house and the kids?"

"You got it," she answered. "You can't even find your underwear. How are you going to prepare meals, wash clothes, clean house and take care of three children? And pity the dog," she concluded, the dare obvious in her voice.

"I fed Mulligan this morning, didn't I?"

"You gave him our supper, leftovers that I had planned to heat up tonight, and then you left him in the laundry room all day. Have you been in the laundry room lately?"

"No, I haven't," I said, a little afraid of what was coming next.

"Well, let's just say that ol' Mulligan did everything in there but fold socks and wash clothes. It wasn't pretty, mister, and I was the one who had to clean it up."

I felt bad about feeding Mulligan leftovers. He was a good dog and deserved better.

Instead, I said in a conciliatory tone, "Honey, I'm sorry about that, but you've got to believe in me a little bit. I can take care of the kids; really I can. And the house, and the dog and start a business. Before long, you'll be able to quit your job and stay at home, too."

She listened quietly, then regarding me suspiciously demanded, "Are you going to raise the white flag the first time you have to change a diaper?"

"I've changed diapers."

"And you've caught fish, too," she said.

"That was ugly."

Turning, she started to walk away, then spun on her heels, and challenged me with, "What do you say we put a little wager on this?"

"You name it," I said, grinning, recognizing a sure thing when I saw it. "But make it easy on yourself."

When she grinned back, her eyes narrowing again, it made me a little uneasy. "Let's say," she offered, "that if you hang in there for 90 days — just 90 — I'll accompany you to Cheap Charlie's golf shop and buy you that new graphite driver that you've been drooling over."

"That would be wonderful," I said, my moment of trepidation fading as my imagination flooded with the thought of whacking a ball 300 yards straight down the fairway. "I really need a new driver. The old one your dad gave me just doesn't connect with the ball right. Because of that dumb club, I accidentally hit an old man the other day."

"You hit a man on the golf course?" Karen asked in disbelief.

"No," I said indignantly. "I didn't hit a man on the golf course. He was driving down the street when I got him."

"That's terrible," Karen said.

"You're not kidding," I said, recalling the incident. "I took a double bogey on the hole. On top of that, when the old guy was released from the hospital, he wouldn't give me my ball back. Now, you know why I need that new club so badly."

"Only if you survive 90 days," Karen reminded me. "If you cave in, you'll have to do the dishes an additional three months."

"Three months all by myself?" I said, trying not to whine. Then, I puffed up and set my jaw like I used to do when I was in the Army. After all, I had commanded a tank company in the First Infantry Division. I could be as tough as the next guy.

"You wash only if you lose," she said. "I doubt that a big, tough, outdoors type like you is going to be beaten by three kids, a tiny house and a collie."

As we shook hands to seal our bet, I thought about winning that new golf club and felt pretty confident. But as Karen turned, I caught a glimpse of her grinning face in the glass, and for a moment, I was clutched by panic. Remembering that I had also been a paratrooper, I was sure that I could be as tough as the next guy, but also just as dumb.

"Naw," I said to myself, "I'll make it."

Chapter 3

Breakfast In Bed

Mother's Day was a bit confusing. I figured that since I was the one manning the home front, it should have been my day. Karen didn't see it that way.

"You've stayed home for two measly weeks and you already think you're a mom," she argued. "For crying out loud, you don't even know how to put away the silverware let alone find the washing machine."

"That's not true," I countered, feeling myself getting a little defensive. "I put a fork away yesterday."

"Forget it, pal," she said, this time grabbing my nose and giving it a little tweak. "I've been the mom around here for years and I'm not about to let you snatch my day away."

So on Mother's Day, Lindsay and I rolled out of bed and huddled together in the kitchen before Karen and the smaller kids woke up. It was to be a meal of uncommon variety in our house. At first, everything went according to plan.

"OK, Lindsay, where do you think we should start?" I asked. Lindsay's a bright kid and a whole lot more knowledgeable about the kitchen and what goes on in there than me.

"I'll start on the cinnamon toast and you cook the bacon," she said with confidence.

"Great," I answered. "Where's the bacon?"

She pointed to the refrigerator, giving me a look that would have made Karen proud.

"Of course," I said. "I knew that. I was just testing you."

"Uh-huh," she said, grinning.

It was amazing how much stuff there was in there. Oh sure, I've looked in refrigerators lots of times. Grabbed a ketchup bottle once or twice, and certainly fetched a beer or two. I'm not talking about that, I'm talking about working out of one. You know, taking stuff and making something with it and then figuring out how to get it all back in. It's a responsibility I never had to deal with before.

There were all kinds of jars, bottles and little plastic bowls with lids on them. I discovered drawers at the bottom jammed with meats, vegetables and baking soda. Unfortunately, there wasn't any bacon and I was about to give up and suggest a quick trip to McDonalds, when I remembered the venison that Uncle Bill had given me a couple of hunting seasons earlier. Knowing what a bad shot Uncle Bill was, I had stuffed it in the back of the freezer, condemning it to road kill.

"You not going to cook Bambi for Mother's Day, are you?" Lindsay gasped when I told her my plan.

"Don't worry," I assured her. "Mom's going to love it — just don't tell her what it is."

While I put the venison into the microwave to defrost, Lindsay worked on the toast. In fascination, I watched as she poured brown sugar into a dish and then mixed it into softened butter. When she was satisfied that the concoction was thoroughly blended, she spread it over hamburger rolls.

"Why not use bread?" I asked. "Wouldn't it be better?"

"Come on, Daddy, it's Mother's Day," Lindsay answered, brushing her thick, red locks out of her face. "We need to use some imagination. Besides, we used all the bread when we went shiner fishing yesterday."

"Oh, yeah," I said, remembering.

When I put the eggs on, I had enough sense not to try to baste them or do anything else that took skill. So I scrambled them using a wooden fork as I had often seen Karen do. When the eggs and toast were at least underway, I went looking for the bed tray.

At this point, I suppose I should mention that breakfast in bed doesn't happen too often in our house, probably because no one has the courage to eat my cooking lying down.

Since I couldn't find the bed tray, I decided to substitute with the kids' play table. I know what you're thinking, even someone as dumb as a husband would know that a play table would be too tall to be functional as a bed tray. But I checked it out by placing it on the couch over my lap. It wobbled a bit, and my nose barely fit over the top, but it was the best I could come up with on short notice.

After testing it, I placed it on the floor in front of me and was about to head back to the kitchen when Lindsay came bursting through the door. Watching her scramble out of the kitchen in a cloud of smoke reminded me of her lovely mother.

"The hamburger buns are on fire," she screeched, "and Bambi's leaking out of the microwave."

I know I should have rushed right in and used my fire-fighting skills. But by that time, however, Tommy was screaming in his room, no doubt having nightmares because of what he had eaten the night before. Not wanting the little guy to waken Karen and ruin her surprise breakfast, I ran to get him instead of into the smoke.

With Tommy in tow, it didn't take me long to get back to the kitchen, but by then the eggs were black, the juice from the deer meat was all over the floor, and Lindsay's cinnamon toast had set off the smoke alarm.

"What kind of doughnuts does Mommy like?" I asked Lindsay when I joined her in the front yard where she had wisely retreated to get away from piercing sounds of the smoke alarm.

"I don't think it really matters," she said.

"Right," I said, "I guess anything would be better than what we have so far."

We went back inside, reset the smoke alarm, then loaded into the car and headed for the nearest doughnut shop.

The clerk's nose twitched when we walked in.

"What's that unusual smell?" she asked.

"Cinnamon," I replied.

"It's more than that," she said.

"And smoke," I added.

"You must be the Pinnocks," she said. "I've heard about you."

My expression must have shown my amazement, because she said, "All the firemen from Stationhouse 49 get their doughnuts here. You're notorious with them."

Looking her square in the eyes, I smiled lamely. "Oh," I said, and then ordered a dozen doughnuts. "Mix 'em up, but no cinnamon."

Surprisingly, Karen was still fast asleep when we returned. No doubt she had heard our efforts in the kitchen and decided to hold out until we served her in bed. Considering it was nearly 11 a.m., I had to admire her determination.

We didn't waste any time as we loaded chocolate, glazed and sugar doughnuts onto the kiddy table. Lindsay added two glasses of milk. I tossed in a cup of instant coffee — I couldn't find the coffee filters — and Tommy paraded in with a stack of napkins and a rose that we had purchased at a gas station. All in all it was a pretty sad-looking breakfast, but better than the one we had left smoldering in the kitchen.

"Happy Mother's Day," we shouted as we carried in the jumbo tray.

Karen immediately sat up, gave us a big smile and then nearly split her sides laughing as she tried to snare a doughnut off the top of the table that towered over her head.

"Maybe we should try placing it on the floor," she said.

"It's OK, honey," I assured her. "I tested it and it's gonna work fine."

"If you say so," she said with a wink.

To this day I'm not sure what happened next. All I know is that one second the table was solidly on the bed and the next, I was reaching to catch it. I missed and breakfast spilled all over Karen, the bed, the carpet, three kids and the dog. If Karen hadn't seen the humor in the bungled ritual, and burst out laughing, I might have cried.

''What's so darn funny?'' I asked, plucking a chocolate dough-nut off Ashley's head.

''Nothing,'' she said, giggling. ''It's just that I can't wait to see what's for lunch.''

Chapter 4

Only Wimps Walk Babies

A s far as I could tell, I was the only househusband on my block. I was pretty sure about that, because each morning as I strolled the children around the block, I saw all of my neighbors hustling off to work. Occasionally, one of them gave me a peculiar look — that goldbrick stare, I remembered from my days in the Army, when I was the one giving it to some suspected slacker. I could almost hear what was going on in their minds; "Get a job, goofball."

The way I had it figured, they thought I was a lazy, no-good bum, who was a couple clubs short of a full set, letting my little wife work while I stayed home. After all, what self-respecting man would spend his time walking a baby?

That macho stuff can really separate a man from a lot of innocent fun. But, at first, I'll have to admit that I was a bit apprehensive about my image as I made the rounds with Ashley and Tommy. It wasn't that I didn't enjoy the walks, I was just worried about what other people would think. Ironically, it was a tough-looking old man, a stranger, who erased my apprehension.

It happened on a weekend that Karen and I had taken the children to New Symrna Beach, a rustic seashore community on the Atlantic about about an hour east of Longwood, where Karen's folks owned a condominium. Since Tommy was in the habit of rising very early, I told my bride that I would get up with him no matter what the hour. Sure enough, on Saturday morning, Tommy woke up at 5:30 and started hollering for something to eat.

Naturally, I didn't hear a thing, but Karen's antenna immediately picked up our son's familiar pre-breakfast squall. Turning a deaf ear to children in the wee hours is a male gift much like the memory bank given to a female in which she can instantly punch up every silly promise made by her husband in a fit of passion. Needless to say, Karen went to the bank and withdrew one sharp jab to the body. When her elbow hit my ribs, it was like a miracle. Instantly, my hearing was restored. Not completely, but enough for me to pick up her next words.

"Do you hear that?" she hissed softly but dangerously in my ear, an amazing ability since none of her words had any esses. In spite of the threat in her voice, it wasn't enough to catapult me into complete consciousness.

In spite of a second lady-like poke, and another small but insistent jibe, my sleep-filled brain resisted total comprehension. "Hear what?" I thought. "A burglar?" I was about to send her downstairs to investigate when Tommy's fussing filtered through.

"It's only Tommy," I announced.

"You promised to get up with him," Karen murmured sweetly, as if that would make up for the bruises forming on my body.

But my memory had been jarred. As I headed downstairs, I silently vowed to be more judicious the next time Karen was accepting IOUs.

Quietly, I fed Tommy, then stuck him in his Batman stroller, and headed for a beach on the Atlantic. No sooner were we outside and walking than I realized I hadn't made such a bad deal after all. It was a magnificent morning; the sun was just beginning to peek over the horizon, a salty breeze was sweeping across the white sand, and there was no one was in sight.

The last was the part I liked the best. Regardless of my love for my son, I still felt like a wuss walking him by myself, and I didn't want anyone to see me. I'm not sure why. Maybe, it's because I never saw Clint Eastwood change a diaper in one of his movies, and whoever heard of John Wayne taking a kid for a stroll. Then,

too, being a Southerner, there are those unwritten male rules regarding propriety and the division of labor between the sexes. I
was beginning to think that the Southern Cross wasn't just a cluster
of stars; it was also all those stupid unwritten rules.

In spite of my unfounded trepidation, I couldn't help but enjoy
myself as we walked along making wheel marks and footprints in
the sand. Tommy was having a ball, drinking in the fishy smells
of the ocean, and watching the pelicans and seagulls drift by
overhead. But after a while, other people began to appear, and I
started growing uneasy again.

Then in the distance, I noticed an older man jogging straight
toward us. As he drew nearer, I could see that he was the kind of
tough-looking bird who would give you comfort if he were leading
you in an attack on an enemy beachhead. Because of that, as he
ran up beside the stroller, I was afraid he was going to make a
wisecrack about what I was doing. Instead, and much to my surprise, he stopped, peeked in at Tommy, and then gave me a friendly
smile.

"I envy you," he said in a voice that fit his image. "I wish I
had taken time to walk my boy when he was young. Now, he's
gone."

Without saying another word, he ran off, leaving me wondering
what had happened to his son, and thankful that I was with mine.
Since then, I've come to realize that there must be other men like
me who enjoy walking their children. Of course, if they're like I
was in the beginning, they'd probably rather eat a jar of strained
peas than confess to that.

For example, I'll never forget the night I was talking and laughing with a group of men at a party when one of them asked me
what I did for a living. If it wasn't for my dishpan hands, I would
have told him that I put out oil rig fires in the Persian Gulf.

Instead, I said, "I stay at home and take care of the kids and the
house."

It was good for a laugh all around, including me.

When the laughing stopped, this guy persisted, "No, Tom, what
do you really do?"

"I'm not joking," I said. "My wife works and I stay at home. I'm starting my own business, so right now, I fill in for Karen and do a little selling off the kitchen table.

For a second, he went slack-jawed, then he slipped off to the kitchen to discuss my status with the others. A few minutes later, I saw him next to a blonde with pouty lips and a blouse a size too small. I heard him say, "See that fellow over there with the red hands, he sends his wife off to work while he stays home and watches ESPN and drinks Budweiser."

I figured he was using me as an excuse to talk to the blonde, and would have ignored him if he hadn't lied. Anyone who knows me will tell you it's the Golf Channel I watch.

Sure, it was just one loud-mouthed jerk, but I'm convinced he's like most men who believe that their wives have the cushiest job in town. A little cooking here, a little ironing there, and the rest of the day for leisure activities.

And while we are usually pretty quick to pat ourselves on the back for the work we do, we seldom appreciate the labors of our loves. I wouldn't admit this to the guys, I mean, if we were standing around and shooting the breeze, but I now realize just how little I did to help Karen with the children and the house. Not only did I never wash a shirt or iron a pair of pants, I never even made a bed or mopped a floor. Occasionally, I did a dish, but only when I had to, and only if it was a little one.

I can remember tossing my clothes around the house, handing her the babies when they fussed, and never lending a hand whenever she prepared a meal — unless, of course, we were cooking outside on the grill.

Why was cooking outside OK? You guessed it: cooking meat over fire is manly and, therefore, fun. Cooking in a pot on a stove is feminine, therefore, unfun.

So when my bride complained about the lack of assistance she received around the house, and that wasn't very often, I did the manly thing. I told her to quit bugging me.

My reasoning, of course, was that I had worked all day, which gave me the right to do what I wanted when I got home.

"After all," I would tell Karen, "you have plenty of time to pick up after me."

I don't believe in ghosts, but stupid things you say to your wife will come back and haunt you every time.

Chapter 5

Never Kiss A Kid Who's Just Eaten A Toad

I could never find the courage to tell Karen about the time Ashley whacked a platoon of toads over the head with her Little Slugger plastic bat and wolfed down a few right in front of my eyes. For some unknown reason — and I'm not ruling out my cooking — little Ashley enjoyed hunting amphibians, reptiles and bugs, then making friends with them before clubbing them into food. No weapon, no problem. She'd squish them with one of her shoes. It was a nasty habit, but it did keep me out of the Gerber aisles at the grocery. Just kidding.

I hate to admit this but she probably picked up this trait to hunt for her food from me, the neighborhood G.I. Joe, a title the kids on the block had bestowed on me. "Start with small game and graduate to the bigger stuff," I thought, smiling over Ashley's skills. For a former paratrooper, this is not easy to admit, but my tiny daughter seemed to have more talent for obtaining wild game than me.

Since I don't want you to think I'm exaggerating, I will relate two incidents that happened within a day of each other. The first occurred after a couple of raccoons terrorized Lindsay's cat, Puppy. That's right, the cat's name is Puppy. In an attempt to get rid of the raccoons, I set a trap baited with chocolate-chip cookies and a bowl of two-percent milk. You can imagine my surprise when, on my first night, I caught two cats, a dog and a neighbor's teen-ager. It was no problem returning the cats and the dog, but the neighbor refused to take back the teen-ager. Well, he finally did accept him, but it cost me $20.

The next day was our toad encounter. In this event, I was Ashley's assistant, kind of like a beater on a small-time tiger hunt. While I scooped, she sat screaming in delight and directing my efforts with her Little Slugger plastic bat.

This incident occurred after one of those heavy rains that seem to punctuate Florida summers. You know the kind I mean: bright sunshine, mysterious cloudburst, more sunshine and enough accompanying humidity to make an alligator sweat.

The two of us had decided to go out for a stroll and, as I hoofed it, she puttered behind me in her walker. In no time at all, we discovered that the storm had washed hundreds of tiny toads out of the swamp behind our house and into the yard. Everywhere we looked, we saw little gray lumps hopping about like popcorn in a hot pan.

Figuring that she might be interested in getting a closer look, I snatched up a few and placed them on the white tray attached to her walker. As I squatted to snare a few more, I heard the unmistakable sound of plastic against plastic. I turned to see her pounding the tray with her Little Slugger. Thinking that this was just a manifestation of the excitement of the hunt, I returned to my scooping.

"Whack, whack, whack," I heard. With no concern about what was going on behind me, I continued to hunt. As I grabbed the toads, I placed them on her tray. Surprisingly, as fast as the capture was taking place, the toads disappeared. Increasing my efforts, I piled them in front of her, but they continued to vanish at an alarming rate. For the life of me, I couldn't figure out what was going on.

"Whack, whack, whack," I heard again, and turned to see the tray empty once more. It suddenly struck me as to what might be happening, and I moved in for a closer look. Much to my horror, I spotted a half dozen little toad feet sticking out of the corner of Ashley's mouth. I was appalled, but she seemed delighted. In fact, as I looked on, her tiny hands swept across the tray, snatching one toad while it was still in the air leaping for safety.

"Spit those things out," I hollered.

Instead of obeying, she turned her head away, popped the toad she had just snagged into her mouth and then scooted off in her walker.

"Come back here, and give me those toads," I ordered in my most fearsome company commander tone, which had the same effect on her as it did on her mother. She giggled and kept on pedaling.

By the time I reached her, all the little feet had disappeared from her lips and not a single one was left on her tray. She grinned up at me and then pleaded in her most winning way, "More hoppers."

"No," I said sternly. "No more toads. And don't tell mommy what you had for lunch."

As distasteful as that little morning stroll turned out to be, it did give me a few good ideas. For example, I found the best way to keep Ashley occupied while I cooked or cleaned was to catch a bug — cockroaches worked best — and let it loose on the floor in front of her. Once she caught sight of the thing, she would usually let out a little yelp and start crawling after it. If she caught it, I stepped in to keep her from stuffing it into her mouth.

Here is another pointer: If you need to distract a little one, and you can't find a good bug, scatter a pack of M&M's or Skittles across the floor. Just pretend that you're feeding chickens or pigs, realizing of course that children are messier. Teaching tots to scramble about the house in search of snacks serves two purposes. First, and perhaps most importantly, it occupies their time. Second, it can help keep your home tidy.

You see, once they have eaten your scatterings, they begin gobbling up other crumbs they come across. When that occurs, be sure to lead them into the kitchen, pointing out the gold mine of goodies usually found under the cabinets.

There is another variation of this game as well. In a home with tots and pets, this centers on living room couches and chairs, which usually have a cache of food under the cushions. Not only does it occupy the child, and save on vacuuming, but it will keep you from having to fix lunch.

All you need is a little imagination and a mom who is not at home. Warning: Try this stuff when she's back at the mansion, and you'll be the one eating food from under the cushions.

And don't forget, tot entertainment doesn't have to be limited to just meal time. This is just a hint, and it usually takes a gifted child to present you with an opportunity like the one I'll soon describe. But remember, most tots have some talent in this area, you just have to be alert to it, and put it to use.

Ashley was a dear, because she had one of those little habits that most parents don't want to talk about; she loved playing in the toilet bowl. Granted, it was nasty, but not without merit.

Instead of going through the frustration of trying to keep her out of the bathroom, I simply bought her a couple of small scrub brushes so that she could clean while she played. Not only did Ashley enjoy herself, but Karen was quick to praise my efforts at keeping our facility spic and span.

More than anything else I came up with, that one bit of inspiration freed me up more time than I can tell you. It gave me the opportunity to develop that little business that everybody was still making jokes about.

I had time for that and to work on my putting stroke, too.

Chapter 6

Can Your Husband Come Out And Play?

When I relate this, you'll probably think that I dove into the shallow end of the pool once too often. Still, I believe my time at home with the Nickelodeon crowd has led me to the fountain of youth. It may sound as crazy as trying to fry a blowfish, but this fountain is a lot easier to locate than some magical spring hidden in a Florida swamp. You see, what I've learned in my time with the kids, was just being around them made me feel and act younger.

I wouldn't have said this before, but I think the guy who sheds his shoes and socks and jumps into a sandbox with his children has a better chance of living longer. If he helps build forts and makes plenty of varoom-varoom sounds as he pushes a toy tractor up a mighty hill, he'll probably be a lot happier, too. The fact is, if we spent less time at the office and more on the playground with the kids, we'd probably have a much stronger family life.

Not only did staying at home allow me to enjoy being with my little ones, but also to spend time with the other youngsters on the block. At first, the neighborhood kids were a bit suspicious of me because they had never been around a stay-at-home dad before. Seeing a man with a mop in one hand and a pacifier in the other was not only scary to my future playmates, but it bewildered the Pakistani neighbor up the street.

"You are a very strange man, very strange," Mr. Chadda said to me one afternoon as I participated with the kids in a brisk game of dodge ball. Since Mr. Chadda was wearing a long dress at the time, I thought his observation pretty funny. Different strokes, I figured. By then, I was kind of getting used to people thinking me weird.

Like the time I was a driver on a field trip for Lindsay's class. We went to the Sanford Zoo — about 15 miles east of Orlando — and all the boys in her room hung out with me because they'd never seen a dad on a field trip before.

"I wanna be just like you when I grow up," one of the boys told me as we watched Maud, an East Indian elephant, celebrate her birthday by devouring a peanut and hay cake.

"How so?" I asked, keeping an eye on Maud as I considered a peanut mix to feed the kids for supper that night. "Hay's out," I thought. "Karen would never stand for it."

The kid said, "I don't wanna work when I grow up either."

"Where do kids get these ideas?" I thought. Looking down at him, I said, defensively, "I work."

"Yeah. Doin' what?"

"Lots of things," I said. When he shrugged and dropped the subject, I remembered Lindsay telling me that the boy's dad was almost never home because of his job. "I work," I mumbled under my breath.

Fortunately, I was strong enough to put such insidious sensations of guilt out of my mind. Then, too, once the kids in the neighborhood learned that I could come out and play when my chores were done, they clung to me like lint. Sometimes, they even pitched in to increase my playtime.

Figuring that it was my duty as an adult to teach cooperation and responsibility, I encouraged their willingness to lend a hand and was always quick to give them a little direction.

"Chris and Bryan, you two put the clean clothes away. Stewart, you vacuum the living room and pick up the stuff on the patio. Adam, you empty the dishwasher. Nabil, you mow the lawn and hose off the patio furniture.

"Gosh, Mr. Pinnock, what are you going to do?" they'd all chime in.

"Are you kidding?" I'd ask in my most astonished tone. "I've got to figure out what kind of entertainment we're going to have this afternoon. Once I do," I said, importantly, "I've got to co-ordinate the recreation facility to match our needs."

For instance, one of our favorite games was cul-de-sac baseball. Instead of a hard ball, we used a tennis ball. That way we didn't need gloves, and the neighbors' windows, cars and small children were fairly safe. Ashley and Tommy were too young to play, so we usually stuck them in the outfield where they crawled around in search of bugs and other appetizers. Lindsay was a dandy little infielder and, like her mom, had a strong right arm.

Bryan's mailbox served as first base, a sewer cover was second and a basketball goal that belonged to Chris — though everyone on the street used it — was third base. On most days, unless it was real hot and everyone was watering their lawns, we'd use a water hose to mark the outfield fence. My job, while the kids were finishing up my chores, was to arrange the water hose.

Fourteen children lived along our block. They came in all shapes, ages, colors and sizes. Among them were the Chadda children. The family had only been in the United States for about a year and knew very little English and nothing about baseball. Still, that didn't keep the youngsters from trying, and it wasn't long before Nabil, Shabista and Humera were picking up American idiomatic expressions faster than the grounders that would scoot through their legs.

Baseball was not their game and they couldn't hit a lick, but it didn't matter to them or anyone else. We were just having a good time, and on those rare occasions, when Nabil, Shabista or Humera did connect, it was fun to see them run the bases in their caftans. So even though their parents were befuddled by the game, the children embraced it.

One afternoon, after Nabil had clubbed one over Shabista's dog, Ninja, who was playing centerfield at the time, I told him that I thought he was going to be the first Pakistani in the Hall of Fame.

"I'd like that very much, Mr. Pinnock," he said with a smile as big as the strike zone as he rounded the basketball goal and headed for home. "What is this Hall of Fame?"

Just because someone doesn't understand a compliment, doesn't mean you shouldn't give one.

On hot days, which during the summer in Central Florida is every day, we'd often trek to a nearby lake where we'd try our hand at catching a fish or two. The kids always expected me to haul in a lunker, figuring that since I was a fishing writer, I'd know how to catch them. After a few expeditions, however, the kids caught on that my fishing talent was on a par with my house-cleaning capabilities.

After one such outing, as we were walking along the lakeshore, Chris looked at me and said, "Boy, we sure did slay them today, didn't we Mr. Pinnock?"

"They were biting," I agreed.

"Yeh," he said, "They were biting so good I had to hide behind a stump so I could bait my hook."

Smiling, he kept on walking, but I could see that he was waiting for a response to his joke.

"You did great," I said, grudgingly.

"Too bad you didn't catch anything, Daddy," Lindsay said with a grin.

"I caught a fish."

"It was a mudfish, Daddy?"

"He put up a fight, didn't he?" I said. "I mean, just before I netted him."

She giggled, then reminded me, "But you didn't net him. He was floating on top of the water, and you used a tree limb to drag him to shore."

"Well, I intended to net him," I said, ready to drop the subject.

But Lindsay was on a roll, and she had an audience in our fishing companions. She said, "Then you kept shouting 'it's a wallhanger, boys, it's a wallhanger.'"

"Well," I said, "it looked big from where I was standing."

Then, my little girl giggled again at the memory of the afternoon, saying ''Daddy'' in that precocious way that precocious little girls have. ''If we hadn't pulled you out of the water after you fell over the wheelbarrow, there's no telling what might of happened.''

''Hey, what was that wheelbarrow doing on the dock anyway?'' I asked as I nonchalantly pulled a minnow out of my breast pocket and flung it back into the water.

''Don't you remember?'' Lindsay said in the way that Karen does when she thinks I'm skirting an issue. ''You said we'd need it to bring back all the fish you were going to catch.''

''Just like her mother,'' I thought. ''Always storing things in her memory bank.''

Chapter 7

Tom Wars

O k, so I was still having a bit of bad luck when it came to fishing, but there were other activities that kept the kids occupied, and I'm proud to say one of them they named after me. *Tom Wars* was a simple little competition. In fact, it was a lot like *Citrus Wars,* except that the oranges and tangerines, which had vanished in Central Florida, were replaced by tennis balls.

Adam, Chris, Bryan, Stewart, Tommy, Lindsay, and whoever else they could recruit into their ranks, made up one team. I was the other. Rule One was to stuff as many tennis balls as you could into your pockets. Rule Two was that senior players could hide balls in various places throughout the battlefield.

I provided the ammunition inasmuch as I had oodles of old tennis balls from the period before I traded in my overhead smashes for cleaning waterglasses. When keeping a tidy house became my game, it was impossible to find time to get to the courts. So, to prevent the balls from becoming moldy, I divided them among the kids for our battle games. Who said that combat training doesn't come in handy in civilian life?

The one other rule for *Tom Wars* was simple. The youngsters would hide and I would look for them. In many ways, the game was similar to hide-and-go-seek, but in this activity the contestants were armed.

As I made my rounds, the pint-sized guerrillas would pop up from behind bushes, fences, cars, dogs or whatever cover they could find, and pelt me with the fuzzy spheres. Anyone hit with a ball was dead. Since I had to be very careful not to nail them too hard, I was dead a lot. As a result, I was often the one who earned most of the style points for dramatic death scenes.

We chased one another all over the neighborhood, tossing balls as we went. When I got behind in my housework, and I couldn't come out and play *Tom Wars,* the children would taunt me from the street.

''Poor little Tom can't come out and play because he's got too much laundry for today,'' they would chant in unison.

Fortunately, I was a grown man, so that kind of teasing didn't make me mad. It made me sneaky. So, as the scoundrels stood in the street bouncing their balls and jeering, I'd creep out the back door with a pocketful of ammunition. Slowly and low to the ground like a paratrooper, I'd crawl around the house, taking advantage of available cover as I went.

Usually, I could get pretty close to the enemy, especially on the days when I took the trouble to slip into my Army fatigues equipped with large, deep pockets, which were ideal for storing balls. Because the camouflage blended in perfectly with the neighborhood foliage, sometimes I could creep near enough to hear them whispering.

''Does anybody see him?'' one nervous warrior would ask another.

Then suddenly, I would burst out of nowhere, flinging balls as I charged forward like an M-1 tank crashing into an enemy line. The children would scream with delight and flashes of joy would streak across their little faces as balls flew past them and me in the exchange that followed.

Tom Wars had begun and they were glad, and so was I, because, as any soldier knows, in the midst of battle, one tends to forget dirty laundry. It was a great game that lasted on and off for about 60 days. Unfortunately, it all came to an end when the moms in the neighborhood complained about finding welts on their children. Occasionally, my enthusiasm for the game got the better of me.

One day, after a particularly tough battle, one of the moms came over and complained to Commander-in-Chief Karen about me smacking her kid in the back with a ball.

"I didn't mean to," I told Karen. "I was shooting for his head."

"You should be ashamed of yourself!" she said in a huff.

"I am," I answered. "I usually have much better aim."

Karen was really angry. I could tell by the way she was holding onto my throat. "No more *Tom Wars!*" she insisted with what I thought was a tad too much pressure on my windpipe. "You're a grown man for heaven sakes. Put the balls away."

From that point on, we replaced the tennis balls with water balloons. I was ashamed that I hadn't considered them before. You couldn't throw the balloons as far, but what they lacked in distance, they made up for in impact. *Tom Wars* was replaced with *Water Wars.* Soldiering is good.

Many great *Water War* campaigns were fought in the streets, in the woods, on the playground and even in a home — ours. But our biggest battle was also our last. So great was this conflict on Eastport Drive that there might be an historical marker there now. It would identify the spot where one of the largest balloon battles and picnics in all of Longwood took place. Everyone on the block got involved — children, men, women, cats, dogs and even a few wild animals that wandered in too close to the action.

Weeks were spent in preparation for the event, including sustenance for the combatants. It was called *Tom's Last War* as I was about to move my family to Atlanta, where I was told that folks who worked out of their homes, be it man or woman, were treated with great respect. For food, each family, including the Chaddas, made their favorite dish. For obvious reasons, I was asked to contribute only the paper plates and cups.

For the battle, each family prepared water balloons, lots and lots of them. It was later estimated that some 2,500 water balloons were thrown that day. Folks in those parts are still talking about it, and a few, I'm told, are still trying to dry out.

Water balloons of all shapes and colors were piled into coolers, wagons, boxes of all sorts, and laundry baskets (I had to dump my dirty clothes out first). Several folks filled their sinks and bath tubs with water bombs. Once the picnic started, the children ate quickly as they were anxious to begin the battle. The teams were simple — kids against adults.

For reasons that seem inexplicable in retrospect, the adults didn't notice when the children slipped away. Perhaps, we were too busy munching on hot dogs and brownies. Suddenly, I heard Jan let out a chilling scream as she took a direct hit from her teen-age daughter. The kid immediately went into a little victory dance, shaking her long blond hair back and forth as she fired off another balloon. Balloons burst all around us and more screams came from the adult ranks as we were caught off guard.

War cries laced with laughter sprang from the throats of the children. They had planned their attack well, and the adults, floundering about, were easy prey. But just when it looked like a slaughter, the adults snatched up balloons and began fighting back.

"Take dead aim," I hollered to my green troops. "Aim low, they're little."

We fought in the streets, in the garages and even in Jan's kitchen. The laughter of the battle was deafening, and the uncontrollable giggles dampened the eyes as much as the water balloons. Before it was over, every man, woman, child and pet was drenched to the bone. Even Mrs. Chadda took part in the fray, though her husband kept a safe distance away.

I heard him say later: "Americans are strange people, very strange,"

"Yes," Mrs. Chadda replied, "but they have much fun."

Chapter 8

Pass the Pepto-Bismol Please

O ne of the most important aspects of running a home is putting meals on the table that are both nutritious and palatable. However, to do this three times a day takes considerable skill, preparation, imagination and luck. For me to accomplish such a feat was nothing short of a miracle. The closest I came was oatmeal for breakfast, hot dogs for lunch and a trip to the Burger King for dinner.

In the past, I took a lot of cheap shots at Karen's cooking. No more. Now that I've had the experience of preparing meals, I realize that cooking for three children and two adults is not that easy. A successful offering can have the same elating effect as a refund check from the government. But bad ones, which are not all that difficult to come by, chip away at one's self-esteem as effectively as a close encounter with a proctoscope.

Since I was the one currently playing with fire, I found the combat boot on the other foot, meaning it was my turn to take a ribbing. Still, being aware that you have some pokes coming, doesn't make them any easier to absorb. Take the time I heard Karen out in the backyard laughing and giggling with Jan, our closest neighbor.

''You wouldn't believe what we had for dinner tonight,'' Karen said over the fence.

''What was it?'' Jan asked.

"I'm not sure, but whatever it was, it was worse than anything I ever served."

"You got to be kidding!" Jan howled.

Karen laughed with her until she realized that she had just taken a hit, too. Fame like flame spreads, and the heat sometimes burns.

But right then, I wasn't thinking about Karen's feelings; I couldn't believe she was maligning what I considered my best culinary effort so far.

"What kind of low-life would make fun of red snapper basted in maple syrup," I thought, pouting. "It was darn good, not to mention healthy."

The truth is, up to that point in my life, I had had very little experience with good cooking. When I first heard the word cuisine, I thought it was a magazine for whiz kids. When my tongue was finally introduced to well-prepared food, the concept of heaven became a reality for me. But that was still years in the future.

In spite of not having an intimate acquaintance with good cooking, I was alarmingly cognizant of table slop. In other words, I knew what was bad, and not just because I had been in the Army. Regardless of how terrible I was in the kitchen, however, many people, preeminently my dad, insist that I wasn't even a contender compared to my mom.

"In a Demolition Derby for food," he would say, "your mom would retire the trophy. She is the best of the worst, a champion of suppertime swill, a woman who could put the word famine into the prayers of a multitude."

And that was when he was feeling eloquent.

At other times, he would assess what was placed on his plate with a simple four-letter word that never makes the crossword puzzles. For years, because of the way he pronounced it, I thought the word had two syllables.

My mom and dad reared seven little Pinnocks. To this day, when we all get together, we marvel at the fact that we managed to survive. Even our pets had enough sense to hunt for their own food.

Mom's meals made it difficult to keep animals around the house, but her tasteless scraps did have some advantages — like no fat people in the family. Also, no roaches scurrying about the house in search of food. In fact, on most mornings, we'd find a dozen or so bugs lying belly up on the kitchen floor. Suicides, we figured.

On the upside, Mom kept a spotless kitchen, and our pots and pans were always in great shape. "Drat!" she'd exclaim as she burned up another skillet. And before I could escape, she'd say, "Check the Sunday paper, Tom. I think I spotted an ad for cookware."

Now, before you get the idea that I used to hang around the kitchen watching Mom cook, I didn't. It was just my bad luck to be passing through during one of her destructive phases, which happened three or four times a month.

Even in the 1950s, when $100 was a pretty good paycheck, it wasn't unusual for us to spend $200 at the grocery, half of which went for new cooking utensils.

"High is the only setting your mom has on the stove," Dad would say. "The next stove I buy is going to come with a flush."

Mom would regard him with good humor, and ask, "What would you like to drink with supper?"

"Pepto-Bismol, my dear," he would respond. "On the rocks."

In spite of an abundance of kidding, none of it seemed to bother Mom in the slightest. I think she knew she was a lousy cook, and may have even taken pride in it.

For all of Mom's culinary shortcomings, the seven of us kids managed to grow up, and, we still joke about what Mom used to do to meat and vegetables and how we couldn't tell them apart. Trying to guess what was on our plate was a popular game in my youth.

If we complained, Dad would talk about all the starving kids in China.

"They go to bed without supper," he'd say. "Lucky kids."

As I explained in the introduction, this was during a period when most chores were assigned by sex. Males did certain things, females did others. So it never occurred to us to lend a hand at the stove. If we had, we all might have benefitted, especially Mom. Preparing food was a responsibility she accepted, but it was never something she did with anything more than a passing interest. Her motto was that if the meat didn't bleed and the vegetables didn't crunch, then supper was ready.

Knowing all this will make it easier for you to understand the mistake I made at 10 o'clock one night when I dropped by my folks' house just before dinner.

"Isn't it kind of early to be eating?" I asked.

"A tad," Mom answered, casually tossing sand on a grease fire. "But I got home early, so I thought we'd eat before the late show."

I was thinking about how I was going to escape the house without hurting anyone's feelings when Dad caught me sneaking out the back door.

"Son," Dad said with a grin, as he moved around me to block the door, "why don't you stay and have a bite to eat."

I knew what he was thinking. He figured if I stayed, there'd be less for him to contend with. I also knew that he liked his dog, Buddy, too much to pawn off any scraps on him.

"I'd love to Dad," I said, trying to get around him, "but I'm afraid I've gotta get Tommy home and put him to bed."

Dad wouldn't budge. He just stood there with a sadistic smile twisting his lips. Then Mom came in.

"Oh, come on, darling," she pleaded. "I've made plenty. Besides, Tommy's not even with you."

I cursed myself for the lousy excuse, poor timing and the meal I saw Mom pull from the smoking stove. When she put the food down in front of me, I stared at it.

"What's wrong?" she wanted to know.

"Is this glob that's moving on my plate the chicken or the macaroni?"

"It's the chicken, darling. Can't you see the feathers?"

On closer inspection, I did spot a couple of charred feathers. I also saw Buddy hightail it out of the house.

"Smart dog," Dad said, whispering to me. "He doesn't want to take the chance of something falling off the table and landing in his mouth."

Somehow, I made it through the evening, although I must say that Dad didn't look too well when I left. I think it was the dessert that got him - leftover sauerkraut smothered in chocolate sauce. Needless to say, I wasn't a bit surprised when Buddy begged to go home with me.

Childhood oaths, usually don't last beyond childhood. But in our family, all seven children have sworn never to allow Mom to cook at family gatherings. It's already producing results: a couple of the kids have gotten fatter, our pets are living longer, and we no longer buy pots and pans after get-togethers.

Considering my early environment and the genetic cooking curse, it stands to reason that what I considered my best meals often ended up buried in the backyard.

"I think this meatloaf is too tough," Karen said after one dramatic presentation that included mashed potatoes with green pepper and banana gravy.

"I can cut it," I said, showing her an edge that I managed to carve off my slice.

"Too tough to stick down the garbage disposal," she said, clarifying her statement, as she brought the meat loaf over to me. "Best bury it deep so no animals can get to it. Wouldn't want them getting sick."

The truth is that before I became responsible for all the cooking in the house, about the only thing I knew how to do was barbecue steaks, chicken and burgers on the grill. The stove was foreign to me, and still is. For that reason, I cooked just about everything outside, which was kind of nice because it helped to keep the house cool during the summer, and it also saved on gas and electricity.

"Since I've been the chief cook and bottle washer," I bragged to Karen, "our electric and gas bills have dropped by more than 20 percent."

As soon as I said that, Karen got out of her chair and left the room. When she returned, she held up a handful of receipts.

"Yeah," I said, questioningly.

"These are last week's receipts for charcoal and lighter fluid," she said.

"Yeah," I said.

"One hundred and one dollars and twenty-six cents."

"Well, everything tastes better when it's cooked outside," I responded, defensively.

Well, almost everything.

There was the time that I tried to barbecue shrimp on the grill. They were so darn small that they kept falling into the flames. In the end, I managed to save a handful, but they didn't taste all that good with bits of charcoal stuck to them.

Wanting to save face after that ordeal, I decided to prepare Karen a special meal: barbecued steak, baked potato, salad and a bottle of wine. I hadn't really shopped for meat before, so you can imagine my surprise at seeing the prices. I settled on a couple of lovely looking pieces of round steak. Those beauties were about half as expensive as the rest, so I knew I had gotten a bargain.

Firing up the grill as soon as I got home, I waited for the coals to burn until they were white, and then flopped on the meat. Earlier, I had tossed in a couple of hefty aluminum-wrapped Idahos. As I was preparing the salad, Karen called from work, and when I told her we were going to have steak for dinner, she got excited and made arrangements to come home early.

I was just taking the steaks off the grill when she zipped into the driveway.

"Everything looks great," she said with undisguised admiration. "When are we going to eat?"

"Don't be in such a rush," I said in the superior fashion of a man who has just conquered the impossible, which in my case was something that we could not only chew but swallow. "This is going to be a meal that you will never forget."

Lindsay and Tommy slid into their chairs, and I strapped Ashley into hers. Karen and I then sat down to a delightful-looking meal. As my bride carefully prepared her baked potato, I passed out the steaks.

"Boy, it sure is great to sit down to a nice meal for a change," I said with obvious pride.

"You're not kidding," Karen answered.

"Can someone help me cut my meat?" Lindsay asked. "I can't put a dent in it."

Calmly, I got out of the chair, walked over to Lindsay, and attempted to cut the meat. After a couple of tough strokes didn't leave so much as a mark, I figured I was hampered by a dull knife. But then I noticed Karen wasn't having much luck with her piece either, which was surprising because she was using the electric knife.

"What kind of steak is this?" Karen asked, sweat pouring off her brow.

"It's round steak," I said. "There's nothing wrong with round steak is there?"

"Round steak," she repeated, and stopped trying to cut it. "Never buy it again until you learn how to cook it."

"And how are you supposed to cook it?" I asked, knowing already that I was going to be offended by her answer.

"The best way is to drop the meat into a pot of boiling water with a cow patty," Karen said. "Then you boil the concoction for about an hour, throw out the round and eat the patty."

"Did you get that recipe from my mom?" I demanded. After brooding for a minute or two, I had to admit that my special meal was a disaster.

Later, when I came into the house after being out for a time, Karen regarded me with what I assumed would be an unspoken question.

"Well?" she asked.

"Well," I answered.

"Did you bury the steaks?"

"I salvaged them."

"How?" she asked. "I used them to hold down the corners of the tarp covering the sandbox."

Chapter 9

Shopping Makes Me Sick

Although cleaning bathrooms, ironing clothes and washing dishes is no picnic, those chores are sometimes a whole lot easier than shopping. Take my last two expeditions, for example. The first took place on a rainy afternoon. I thought it would be nice to spend some quality time with my little buddy, Tommy, and since he had been bugging me for a rubber snake, I decided to take him to the Altamonte Springs Mall, which is one exit south of Longwood on Interstate 4.

Our first stop was at a candy store, where we purchased a sackful of chocolate-covered almonds, a weakness of mine. Chocolate-covered almonds are a frailty that I'm willing to share most of the time. But from experience, I know I have as much chance of sampling one once they reach the house as I do of winning back-to-back state lotteries. So it was out of pure greed that we made that purchase before doing the rest of our shopping.

I know this sounds like a cliche, but my mouth was watering at the thought of those treats when I strapped Tommy in on the passenger side. Then I goofed. I left the candy on the seat next to him as I walked around the front of the car to the driver's seat. I mean, at the outside, how long could that take? Ten seconds? Fifteen seconds. By the time, I got in and fastened my seat belt, Tommy had wolfed the lion's share of the chocolate faster than Ashley could down a toad. The rest looked like skid marks on a rabbit farm.

Tommy held out two for me. As soon as I looked at them, I lost my taste for chocolate-covered almonds and shook my head. "No thanks, little buddy," I said, then put the car into gear and started to wheel out of the parking lot. I paused to let an old man in nothing but walking shorts and white sneakers go by. I think it was a little old man, but it's not always easy to tell in Florida.

"There sure are a lot of people here today," I said to Tommy, casually flicking away a hefty particle from under his nose.

"What was that, Daddy?" he asked as he gobbled up the candy he had offered me, testing my gag reflex.

"A booger," I answered, absently.

"Oh," he said, "I like to wipe those on the TV."

Yep, a man and his boy shopping, which meant no running from one store to the next in search of shoes, pantyhose or dresses. No abrupt stops to examine sales items. No impromptu side trips for makeup and those embarrassing items that women make men buy when they want to torture them. Instead, we sampled the best that the snack bars had to offer, browsed through the bookstores and tried out a number of golf clubs at Sears. We figured if we had time, we'd visit the pet shop to check out the puppies. But first, we had to buy a rubber snake.

By the time we entered the toy store, Tommy was quiet. Too quiet.

"I don't feel so good," he said. "Hold me?"

"Sure thing," I said, picking him up. "Don't worry, we'll find you a snake. A great big one, too."

Between the time we left Sears and arrived at the toy store, it had started to rain, and people crowded in everywhere. As a result, the toy store was packed. Wild-eyed kids were romping down the aisles honking this, squeaking that and making rat-a-tat sounds that combined to create a cacophony that would give a busy New York street a run for its money in a noise-pollution test. For the parents, their task was like trying to grab a loose firehose. Just thinking about it again makes my eyes blur.

But I was on a mission, so, carrying Tommy in one arm, I slithered through the crowd searching for the rubber snake section.

Finally, I spotted just the item I thought Tommy would want. It was next to a couple of gray-haired matrons who were intent on a conversation they were having with a talking stegosaurus. Squeezing into the area beside the women, I reached out to gather in the rubber viper.

To do so, I braced myself with the hand that was supporting Tommy in my arm, and leaned in. It was at that precise moment, that this horrendous retching sound emerged from my little boy. Wishful thinking, I suppose, made me suppose that it was coming from a stack of toy dinosaurs just above my head. But then, I heard the women scream, and I knew the truth. I looked at Tommy just in time to see him give up his lunch all over me and the women. The mixture of chocolate-covered almonds, hot dog and soda was not a pretty sight. It was enough to stun the women momentarily, and to mortify me. Before the women began screaming again and pointing in my direction, I bolted.

I know what I should have done, and as I moved swiftly toward the safety of the mall's inner court, I considered going to the manager and seeing if he could give me some rags, towels, mop, bucket and a dozen volunteers to clean up the mess. That's what I should have done. However, I abandoned that idea before it had time to lodge in my brain, then glanced around to see if there was a restroom where I could at least rinse off the stuff covering Tommy's shirt and half of mine. But just then, I spotted what looked like a security man about the size of an NFL tackle closing in on the screams, and I dashed from the store into the mall's inside courtyard.

It wasn't my most honorable move, but Tommy was turning greener by the second, and I didn't feel all that well myself. Fear gripped me. Not that I thought there was anything seriously wrong with the boy, but I was certain that at any moment he would release another shot of the mixture.

As we raced by shoppers in the courtyard, I heard one little girl say, ''Did you see that, Mother? They were gross.''

''Don't look, honey.''

''They stink, Mother.''

"I know, dear."

In my anxiety to flee, I took a wrong turn. So instead of heading for the exit and the rain-drenched parking lot, I moved toward one of those temporary sales stations — a cosmetic counter — that had been set up in a wide area between the stores.

As luck would have it, I had just entered into a crowd of women gathered around the station. They were listening to a saleslady who looked as if she had just spent the morning with Elizabeth Taylor's makeup artist.

"I don't feel so good, Daddy," Tommy said.

"Clear the way," I bellowed as I tried to push my way through the crowd. My warning came too late. Tommy gave me my very first look at projectile vomiting. It hit the glass-top counter, sprayed upwards and outwards like soggy buckshot catching the saleslady and the customer on whose wrist she was spraying perfume.

The salesgirl reeled back in disbelief as the surprised customer quickly put a hand to her mouth. I didn't stick around. Finding an exit, I dashed out into the cover of the dounpour and quickly loaded Tommy into the car.

As we drove away, Tommy said, "I feel much better now. Did you get my snake?"

"No," I said, "and I don't think we'll be coming back here for a while."

"When, Daddy?"

"When you're 21, son. Maybe later."

It was several weeks before I dared show my face in the mall again. I rationalized that if I combed my hair and wore something very clean and very white, no one would ever suspect me as the spew king.

Considering that it was the night before Karen's birthday, I had to chance it, and decided to take the children shopping so they could get Karen a gift. Not wanting to gamble on us buying her something stupid, Karen decided to come along.

"No more cheap perfume and jewelry," she said as we headed into the mall. "I'd rather have a mop."

A mop was something I hadn't considered, and might have gone for it if I hadn't picked up on the sarcasm in her voice. So instead, I did the husbandly thing and became defensive.

"Cheap," I countered. "Those last earrings cost me nearly three bucks, and everyone knows that Tattoo ain't that cheap."

"Tabu," she said.

"Why can't we discuss this?" I asked.

"Tabu is a perfume," she said, glancing at me sideways to see if I was really as stupid as I sounded. "Tattoo is something that men do to make themselves uglier."

"Oh," I said, growing nervous as we got out of the car and headed for the stores, retracing some of the same steps that Tommy and I had taken on our last trip. At any moment, I half expected someone to leap out and scream, "There they are. Those are the creeps who trashed our store and slimed our customers."

Fortunately, nothing like that happened, and after a while, I began to relax as Karen fingered dresses and bathing suits in the deliberate way that a woman has that forces her husband to look for a place to sit. There was a backless bench and I joined two other guys and quickly assumed the 100-yard stare, looking into space at nothing. Occasionally, I'd see Karen scurrying about, tucking dresses and blouses under her chin, in a dash for the changing rooms. Right on her heels was Lindsay, soaking up her mother's techniques, emulating her every move. It reminded me of a TV show I saw about a lioness teaching her cub to hunt.

As I watched the two of them zip through the women's section of the department store, I realized that this was the very training that a boy doesn't get. It's no wonder that it takes me an hour to buy diapers at the grocery store — I didn't get the proper training.

While the females in the family continued their gathering, Tommy and I hung back and played hide-and-seek amongst the rows of clothes. We were having a terrific time, too, until he began to slow down and complain about not feeling well.

"My tummy hurts, Daddy."

Strange as it may sound, I wasn't the least worried.

"Naw," I reasoned. "It's a million to one that he'd get sick in the same mall two times in a row.

"Daddy, can I sit in the stroller?"

"Sure," I said as I lifted him into the seat.

"I don't feel so good," he said.

Those words struck terror in my heart. "You're going to be fine, little buddy," I said, encouragingly. "You probably feel a little bad because you lost those last two games of hide-and-seek."

He tried to smile, but his lips wouldn't part. His eyes were half closed and his face began to turn white. I spotted Karen and quickly wheeled over to her.

"I think you better take a look at Tommy. He says he's not feeling well."

Karen laid down an armful of dresses and felt Tommy's head. "We need to get him home," she said. "He's running a fever."

We placed Karen's selections back on the rack and bolted for the parking lot, where we quickly loaded the stroller and the children into the car. Tommy sat up front next to me.

"I wanna be close to my Daddy," he mumbled.

As soon as I pulled out of the parking lot, Tommy complained again.

"Do you think you'll be all right until we get home?" I asked him.

I don't know what I was thinking. I should have just taken him out of the car and walked a little ways to a grassy spot. But this came to me too late. Before I could do a thing, he let go with the same kind of fury that he had shown in the toy store. Once again, I had been thoroughly slimed.

Pulling the car off the busy road, I helped Tommy out of the front seat. As I was attempting to clean him off with a bundle of baby wipes, he looked at me and said, "Daddy, I don't like shopping. It makes me sick."

Chapter 10

In The Pink

Boy, is my face red. Just when I thought I was getting a handle on this homemaking business, I go out and do something really dumb. From the start, I was warned that one of my toughest duties would be keeping up with the dirty laundry. Frankly, I couldn't see that this task was such a big deal. After all, we had a washer and dryer; it wasn't as if I had to go down to a stream and beat the stuff against a rock.

As it turned out, I'd probably have been better off doing just that. The first thing I learned was that you can't just pick up clothes and toss them in the washer. First, you have to search them out from atop shelves, under beds and behind doors. And it didn't matter how often I lectured the kids and my bride on the subject.

"Put your clothes in the laundry basket," I begged a million times. "You know, it's that round plastic thing in the laundry room — the one that's always empty because nobody uses it."

I can't remember when it started, but every time I'd begin a harangue, the kids would become a trio to chorus, "Lecture, lecture" altogether. Even Ashley. In fact, those might have been her first words after she said Mommy. I'm not sure now, but it must have been my approach to talking about problems, because I'd see Karen tell the kids what they were supposed to do, and they would do it.

Anyhow, you get the idea; I might as well have been talking to heads of cabbage for all the good my pleas were doing me. To make matters worse, in my mind, the appeals seemed to encourage everyone to dirty more clothes and find trickier places to hide them. It was a losing battle that made me want to tie their underwear in knots.

And it didn't get any easier once the clothes were gathered. Indeed, I quickly realized there was a lot more to getting clothes clean than I had ever imagined. For example, there was that business about separating whites from colors.

Oh sure, I could go through a pile of laundry and put all the white stuff in one stack and all the brightly colored stuff in another. My dilemma was that once I'd finished doing that, there remained a third pile that didn't fit into either category. The in-betweeners. After a few weeks, however, it was a predicament that resolved itself. By that time the in-betweeners had disappeared. I still had three piles, but now they consisted of whites, brightly colored stuff and pinks.

I know you are going to say that you could see that one coming. But in my defense, let me explain that like any self-taught artist of note, my pink period in the laundry room occurred before my education was complete, meaning before I was introduced to the value of proper temperature settings.

I'm much smarter now, since I learned about hot wash, warm rinse; warm wash, cold rinse; cold wash, cold rinse; and my favorite — no wash, no rinse. Who would have ever thought that clothes were so fussy about their water? What I needed was a washer as smart as my camera.

Many cameras today can take one look around, measure the available light and then automatically focus on a subject before you can say cheese. Now, if engineers can figure that one out, why can't they invent a washing machine that can examine the clothes in its tub and determine what kind of water and how much detergent are needed to wash them properly?

With one of those babies, my life as the lord of the laundry room would have been much simpler and my family would have worn a lot less pink. More importantly, such a machine would have saved me from one of life's most embarrassing moments.

That incident took place my second week on the job. It was precipitated because of a day in which I was in a hurry. In an effort to save time, I didn't sort anything. Instead, I stuffed a heaping pile of clothes, towels, sheets and sneakers into the washer. I glanced at what I was washing, but didn't examine the clothes closely. Even worse than that oversight was the one regarding temperature setting. I had left it on hot wash, warm rinse.

When I opened the washer lid sometime later, you can imagine my horror on discovering that all the whites had turned pink. One by one, I picked each item from the washer's tub and finally found the culprit, which was Ashley's little fuzzy red shirt. It emerged looking as anemic as a failed suicide.

Sorting through the mess, I convinced myself that the situation did not compare to such disasters as Pompei or the Black Plague. So what if the white sheets and towels were pink. Karen likes pink, Lindsay likes pink, even Ashley likes pink. I decided that I would like pink, too, even red, considering the fact that the Soviet Union had finally succumbed to reality.

It was at the precise moment that I was waxing philosophical that I spied my underwear. When I held up a pair for examination, I was pretty sure that they had been white before they went into the water.

Looking at the rest, I quickly calculated how many pairs I had that were still white. I sighed, remembering. ''One,'' I said aloud. It was the pair I was wearing. Then, with my luck for getting caught in situations at precisely the worst time, Lindsay walked in as I was raging through all of my briefs, trying to pretend they weren't really as pink as they were.

''I thought only girls wore pink underwear,'' she said, giggling.

Turning, I gave her my most threatening frown, and she fled from the laundry room.

When Karen came home and discovered what I had accomplished, she was equally amused, especially when I related that the only white briefs I had left were the ones I had on.

With that piece of information, her smile widened into laughter that soon had tears streaming down her face.

"You want to model them for me, big boy?" she asked in a lousy imitation of Mae West.

When I frowned at her with the same kind of threatening intensity that had sent Lindsay scurrying, Karen only laughed harder.

"Hee, hee," I said. "But you might as well forget it because pink will never become a permanent part of my ensemble. I'll never wear them. Never. Not in a million years. Not if they were the last pairs of men's underwear on the planet."

With Karen enjoying herself so much, Lindsay joined in on the festivities, and then Ashley. Ashley didn't know what was going on, but if Mommy and her sister were laughing at me, it must be the thing to do. Tommy laughed, too, but he didn't have a clue as to what was occurring until Lindsay and Ashley began dancing and hooting and waving my pink Fruit of the Looms over their heads. That was a game he could really get into, and did.

When the kids finally quieted down, Karen looked at me playfully and said, "Gosh, honey, I think you'd look adorable in pink unmentionables. Maybe you could dye your T-shirts and socks to match."

That was enough. I snatched up my briefs and tossed them into the garbage, foolishly thinking that that was the end of it.

Several days later, I was putting away some clothes, when much to my horror, I discovered a pair of my pinkies hiding under a covey of mateless socks.

"OK, who's the wise guy?" I asked Karen and the girls, who were sitting in the kitchen chomping on giant cookies to keep from laughing. "Which one of you is responsible for this?" I demanded.

They met my pique by peeking from behind the cookies and giggled some more.

I knew I was the victim of a female conspiracy. Conspiracy to do what, I couldn't fathom, but I knew it was a conspiracy. But by then, I had gone to the mall and purchased a half dozen new pairs. So I knew I was safe.

"OK, very funny," I said, "but just remember, in this lifetime, I'll never wear these sissy shorts."

Two days later, I got sick. When I awakened that morning, it felt as if a sharp knife had been stuck in my throat and that my stomach was stuffed with crab grass. All I wanted to do was lie in bed, which turned out to be impossible. After my third inconclusive trip to the bathroom, I was convinced that I was on my way to that big laundromat in the sky.

When I whined about my condition to Nurse Karen, she regarded me sympathetically and said in her best bedside manner, "Don't be so dramatic. Your problem is nothing more than the unpleasant after-taste of your own cooking."

"That's pretty low," I moaned.

"I told you," she said, "chew, don't swallow."

"You're a nurse," I wailed. "Here I am facing death and you're taking cheap shots."

For a moment, she relented, remembering, I suppose, that men can't take pain without the comfort of mothering. "Your temperature's not that high," she said, soothingly. "I know you've been throwing up all over the dirty sheets, but that's no reason to think you're going to die."

"I hurt," I said.

"I know," she replied. "Now stop your whimpering and get dressed so I can take you to the doctor's office."

Quickly, I pulled on some clothes in the darkened bedroom and went outside to crawl into the front seat of the car, where Karen was already waiting.

"Now, darling," she said, patting me on the head as if I were a little boy. "If you're going to barf, let me know so I can slow down. I don't want any of that stuff blowing back into the car."

Since I was feeling sorry for myself, and she wasn't taking me seriously, I couldn't keep my lip buttoned. So I shot back, "What a joke! The 1st Division could puke in your car and you'd never know the difference. Not the way you keep it."

Considering my condition, that was a really stupid comment. No sooner had I made my observation than Karen put the car into the oops mode. A moment later, we flew around the next corner on two wheels in a maneuver that had Coke cans and a flight of plastic toys richocheting off the dashboard and into my head. It also had my stomach flipping up towards my mouth. Quickly, I rolled down the window in an attempt to aim away from the front seat.

After I had given up the rest of last night's Spam a la Tom, I began complaining. "Don't take me to the doctor," I begged. "Take me to the morgue."

"Men are such babies," my bride hissed as she whisked the car into a parking space. When she hissed this time, at least, she had some esses to work with.

As I walked into the waiting room, feeling that I was looking as pathetic as I felt, the nurse announced that it would be at least 30 minutes before the doctor could see me. As bad as I was feeling, this news was almost too much to bear. Nevertheless, it wasn't out of meanness but desperation that made me blurt, "I think I'm going to give up my breakfast."

It wasn't a threat mind you. But the effect was the same as if I was holding a hand grenade with the pin pulled. The nurse jumped up, threw open the door to the waiting room, grabbed me by the shirt and dragged me toward an empty examination room.

"Aren't you coming with me?" I asked Karen, who was busy ripping out coupons from a Good Housekeeping magazine. If I hadn't been feeling so bad, I might have chuckled. My housekeeping had been so bad that the magazine canceled our subscription.

"No, go ahead, honey," she said. "You're a big boy."

The room the nurse pushed me into reminded me of a closet, only smaller. In the center was a pint-sized bed covered with white paper that crackled every time I moved. The examination room was different from others I had been in only because there was a toilet attached.

"If you have to," the nurse said, pointing to the toilet, "do it in there."

I nodded silently.

As the nurse left the room, she didn't quite close the door behind her, and I heard her mumble, "Can't be too sick if he had breakfast."

A few minutes later, I overheard the doctor talking to the nurse in low tones. "You look terrible," he said to her.

"The reason's in there," she said, nodding in the direction of my room. I caught a glimpse of her expression, which indicated she considered me a wimp. It was almost enough to make me stop crying and remove the pillow from under my arm.

The doctor was friendly enough. After all, he was a man and could understand male suffering. He did make me put the pillow down, however.

After sticking what felt like a two-by-four down my throat, pulling on my ears, and placing a cold stethoscope on my chest, he instructed the nurse to give me a shot of penicillin.

"I knew I was really sick," I thought triumphantly. "Wait till I tell Karen. She'll feel sorry for the way she acted."

It felt good to be right, but so deep in thought was I over this meager moment in the catbird seat that I didn't hear the nurse's first request.

"What?" I asked.

"Drop your drawers," she ordered as my new friend, the doctor, disappeared, closing the door behind him.

Unfastening my belt, I let my pants slip down around my ankles. No sooner had I done so than the nurse began to laugh. Not a polite, little chortle, either, but rather a deep belly-wrencher that echoed around the tiny room.

Looking around at her in what was the beginning of anger, I followed her gaze to my shorts. My pink shorts. Ugh! I didn't even feel it when she drove the needle up to the hilt into my backside.

Chapter 11

Sorry, Wrong Number

T he dishwasher backed up and spit up all over the clean floor, the washing machine got stuck on rinse, Ashley pulled an electric can opener down on her head, Lindsay stayed home from school with the flu, and Tommy killed his pet turtle, Spud. He claimed he accidentally backed over him with his Big Wheel. All in all, it was just another morning at 516 Eastport Drive in Longwood.

The really exasperating part in all this was that everything happened on the same day before noon. To make matters worse, I could tell my mental attitude was on a downslide. It wasn't just that Karen and the kids were suggesting that folks in famine-plagued countries were eating better than we were, but that their living conditions were probably superior, too. At least, cleaner. On top of that, after all the good-natured laughter at my expense over the laundry and my pink shorts, they were upset about the tint of their own clothes. For a time, it seemed as if my dog was the only loyal friend I had left, and then he began spending more time next door, too.

I also lacked privacy. Even when I retreated into the bathroom, Tommy was close behind pounding on the door.

''What are you doing, Daddy?'' Tommy would ask.

''Nothing, son.''

''Then, can I come in?''

''No, I'm reading a book.''

"I thought you said you weren't doing anything?"

"I'll be right out," I said.

"You better hurry, Daddy. The phone's ringing."

The phone! I hadn't answered the phone in my house in months, because to beat Lindsay to it, a person would have to be an Olympic runner. For some reason, my children seem to think it's their duty to get to the caller first. They scream, beg, and brawl for the receiver. They're like piranha fighting over raw meat. And yet, when they finally hand the phone over to me, they don't have a clue as to who's on the other end.

"It's for you, Daddy."

"Great. Who is it?"

"I don't know."

"Is it a man or a woman?"

"I'm not sure."

"Is it an animal?"

"Oh, come on, Daddy. You know animals can't talk."

"How about Mickey Mouse?" I said.

By the time I picked up the receiver, the caller usually would hang up. Unless, of course, it was a salesman. They never hang up, give up, or take no for an answer.

"Mr. Peacock?" a salesman asked.

"The name is Pinnock."

"Oh, I'm sorry, Mr. Pinhick. I'm with Arctic Air-conditioning Service, and we have a super deal going this month. If you agree to have one of our technicians come out, we'll service your unit, check all its parts, trim your bushes and paint your house."

"Paint my house, trim my bushes? I thought you said you were in the air-conditioning business?"

"We are. Those are just a few extras that we like to throw in to show you that we care. We do care Mr. Pinhead."

"The name is Pinnock, and how much is your caring going to cost me?"

"That's the exciting part. There is absolutely, positively no charge for parts and labor. There is, however, a small service charge."

"How small?"

"Oh, we can't discuss that over the phone, but I can assure you that we have an easy-payment plan that can be stretched out over a 30-year period."

"Thanks, but my mother overhauled the unit last week."

And if it wasn't the heater and air-conditioning people, it was the carpet beggers.

"Mr. Peanut, this is..."

"The name is Pinnock."

"Golly, I sure am sorry about that Mr. Pignet. As I was saying, I'm Pete Tack with Miracle Carpet Cleaning Inc., and we have a special this week that you can't afford to turn down. For only seven dollars and nineteen cents, we'll clean all the carpets in your house, your neighbor's house, and, just to show you that we're one whale of a company, we'll even wash your dog. You do have a dog don't you, Mr. Pinhock?"

"The name, Mr. Tacky, is Pinnock, and though some folks don't think Mulligan is much of a dog — he never did learn to lift up his leg when he tinkled — in my opinion he's a pip of a pup. By the way, what's the catch?"

"Oh, there's no catch, Mr Pinuck. We simply require you to sign a service agreement that allows us to clean your carpets twice a year for the next 50 years.

"Thanks, Tacky, but I have wooden floors."

"You mean you don't want the service?"

"That's right, I don't want your service."

"Fine, but let me tell you something Mr. Penhook, you really need to do something about your dog."

The biggest problem with the interruptions was that they put me behind on my housework. I don't know what was worse, the annoying salesman or the kids continually tugging on my sleeves. Karen was no help either. I couldn't begin to remember the last time she took me out to a peaceful dinner or a movie.

For that matter, I couldn't recall the last time I had a conversation with someone taller than a laundry basket. Maybe that's the reason

I lost my ability to communicate. Furthermore, unless the conversation was about the rising cost of diapers, or how to wax a floor without leaving streaks, I was as out of place as a firefighter in a rain forest.

And all of this had happened to me in less than three months. "How in the world do people do this stuff for a lifetime?" I asked myself.

That's when I called my mom for advice. Now, there was a super mom. She reared seven children and took care of a house and a dog. "Eight kids," she was fond of saying, "when you count your father."

"Hi, Mom, how are you doing today?" I asked.

"Who's this?"

"It's Tom, Mom."

"Tom who?"

"Tom, your son. You know, the fella who used to cut your grass."

"Oh sure. I remember you. You're the one who's staying home with the children while your poor little wife goes to work. I always knew there was something peculiar about you."

"Well, that's what I wanted to talk to you about, Mom. How in the world did you do it?"

"Do what?"

"Have seven kids?"

"Say, if you don't know how that works by now, you're not only peculiar, you're backward."

Good ol' Mom, always poking fun at people. Boy, am I glad I didn't grow up to be like that. "You know darn good and well what I'm talking about," I said. "You must have some tips, some bits of wisdom to pass on that would make it easier to take care of the kids and to do the housework."

There was a moment of silence, followed by a strange little laugh. "Oh sure, I remember those days."

"Well, what did you do to keep from going crazy?"

"Son, anyone who has seven kids is a little crazy, but no crazier than a lazy scoundrel who gives up a good job to loaf around the house. You ought to be ashamed of yourself. I taught you better than that.''

''Mom, quit kidding. You must have some suggestions so I can cope, something I could do that would help.''

''Well, now that you mention it, Tim, my lawn could sure use a good mowing.''

Chapter 12

Be All That You Can Be

I used to look forward to seeing the little white mail truck zooming through our neighborhood each day. It wasn't because I was expecting anything important, I simply enjoyed chatting with someone who was over three feet tall and didn't have juice stains around his mouth. As luck would have it, the mail carrier turned on me, too.

"You'd be surprised how much better you'd feel if you brought home a paycheck once in a while," he growled at me one morning.

His tone had the consequence of ice on warm flesh. I was startled, then angry, and for a moment, I considered making fun of his ridiculous-looking safari hat and hairy knees. Biting my tongue, I decided that he was probably jealous because it was 2 in the afternoon and I was playing baseball with a bunch of kids. Besides, any retort I might have made was impeded by the mouthful of Skittles that I was passing from cheek to cheek in a candied imitation of a Big Leaguer.

"Hey," I finally said as I gulped down the last batch, "I thought you knew that I was a stay-at-home dad working out of my house."

Regarding me with undisguised contempt, he shoved a heap of letters and bills into my hands, and then sped off in the Jeep, yelling out the window as he turned the corner. I couldn't quite make out what he had to say, but I was pretty sure it had something to do with fertilizer.

"Oh yeah," I screamed after him, giving him my best retort. Then, I said, more quietly, "Shave your knees, you big geek."

As I waited for my time to bat, I quickly glanced through the mail, spotting a letter from the United States Army addressed to Captain Thomas W. Pinnock.

Just seeing my name and rank on that envelope lifted my spirits like a kite in a March wind. They didn't rise straight up, but flopped around a little like a kite when it's gusting and you're not sure which way the wind will blow.

"Yesiree, Bob," I murmured, trying to rid myself of that bit of anger that was still nagging at me. "Let that mail creep think what he might, but right here is proof that I wore a government uniform once, too, and I did it in long pants."

By then, I had been out of the Army for nearly five years, but I was still in the Army Reserves and considered myself a highly trained fighting machine. A little rusty to be sure because of all the dishwater I had been dipping into, but a machine nonetheless. Clutching the letter close to my apron, I double-timed (Army talk for ran) into the house.

"I'll be back in a minute," I assured my fellow ballplayers. "I just got a letter from the Army."

I couldn't imagine what the Army wanted with me, but at that moment, I would have volunteered for a dangerous mission to some remote jungle or far-away island. Even a place overrun by communist guerrillas. Or bandits. Or whatever they're called these days.

Army intelligence being as efficient as it is, they undoubtedly knew the terrific odds I had been up against in the past few weeks.

Hope will do that to you. It adds adrenaline to the imagination, and I could picture a high-ranking general saying, "If that young captain can handle three kids, a dog and a working wife — not to mention a snotty mail carrier — we need him in the trenches."

So it was with a great deal of anticipation that I tore open the envelope and began reading:

"Dear Captain Pinnock:
We regret to inform you that because of recent military cutbacks, we
will no longer need your services in the United States Army Reserves..."

"RIFfed," I shouted, nearly falling out of my sneakers. "I've been RIFfed."

I had read about the reduction in force that all the Armed Forces were going through, but somehow, I never expected it would affect me. My specialties were still key ingredients even in a reduced Army.

I was enraged. "Fighting machine," I said. "Now, I'm nothing but a washing machine."

Didn't those administration geeks at the Pentagon — the same ones who couldn't tell the difference between a submachine gun and a submarine sandwich — know that I was the toughest paratrooper ever to come out of the southside of Altamonte Springs? What the heck was going on here?

The shock of it threw me right back into my macho thinking. "The military was ashamed of me," I decided. "I had become a homemaker, and the brass didn't want their tank commanders washing clothes, changing diapers and taking walks with toddlers in strollers."

Then I wondered if someone had seen me playing in the sandbox with Tommy, and reported that my varoom-varooms seemed a little squeaky to them.

Most men probably would have been thrilled with such a letter from the Army, but to me at that very moment, it was as emasculating as if I had had my ears pierced and had just made an appointment for a bleach job.

Quicker than the anger had come, it disappeared, and I began to laugh at myself.

"They obviously don't know what a terrific job of soldiering I had been doing in Central Florida," I thought, grinning. With that in mind, I sat down at the typewriter and wrote a letter to the Big Brass in Washington DC.

Dear Sir:

Yes, it is true that Captain Thomas W. Pinnock, a former tank commander and paratrooper in your fine army, is now a househusband. You may, as so many have, find this humorous, but certainly not enough to boot me out of the ranks. You've got to know that taking care of a houseful of kids is a lot like war, only tougher.

Indeed, general, have you ever tried to wheel two kids in a stroller through a crowded mall? It's more difficult than belly crawling through a minefield. Have you ever tried dining with three little ones at a Chuck E. Cheese Pizza on a rainy Saturday afternoon? I'd rather eat cold C-rations for Thanksgiving dinner.

Furthermore, general, since I've been holding down the fort here in Central Florida, not one enemy army, or for that matter, one enemy soldier, has taken a foot of ground in this area. That's right, sir, not only have I helped to keep the enemy hordes at bay, but since I've been here, the Warsaw Pact has crumbled like a cheap doughnut, and the Iraqi army has given a whole new meaning to the word "retreat."

Sir, my record speaks for itself. I'm as tough to get rid of as a chocolate stain on a little girl's blouse, and to cut me loose like an unwanted catfish is an injustice. Besides, I can bake some terrific cookies. Please take the time to reconsider, and let me know what kind of cookies you like.

Sincerely,
TWP

If I had stayed angry, I might have sent that letter. And I know the general would have appreciated my chocolate puffs. Oh well, at least the Army taught me a lot, and the training certainly came in handy around the house.

When the kids learned about the RIFfing, it was Lindsay who spoke up. "Gosh, Daddy," she said, "does that mean we don't have to salute you when you come into our room now?"

"Right," I replied.

"And does that mean an end to morning inspections?"

"You got it," I answered, "but I still expect spit-shined shoes for church and bedspreads so tight I can bounce quarters off the top of them. We'll also continue laundry practice."

"Do we have to?" Lindsay and Tommy chimed in unison.

"You bet. We're going to run a tight outfit around here in your mother's absence. Wouldn't want her to think we were slacking off, would you?"

"Mom was never in the Army," Lindsay said, "and things went OK when she was in charge."

"Insubordination," I said, "and you know what that could mean."

"You mean I'd have to clean the latrine with a toothbrush again."

"Gotcha," I said, grinning.

Lindsay grinned back. "The last time you had me do it, I used your toothbrush."

It isn't exactly with nostalgia that I look back at my Army days, but I can see where my service time prepared me for working around the house. For instance, at Fort Knox, Kentucky, where I went to boot camp, my drill sergeants taught me how to fold socks, mop floors, and peel potatoes. They also instilled in me survival techniques on a modern battlefield, which are similar to those at home.

Even when I was a little squirt, Dad showed me how to do dishes the Army way. As I recall, it went something like this: Fill one sink up with soap and scalding hot water. Fill the other sink up with scalding hot water. Wash the dishes in the scalding soap side and rinse them in the scalding water side.

"Don't be a coward," Dad would bellow. "Plunge your hands in there and fetch those forks."

"Yeowwww, Daddy! That's hot."

"Darn tootin'," the old Army Air Force captain would chuckle. "No germs can live through that."

Never let a towel touch a dish was his motto. Dad said there were too many germs on towels. Instead, he had us set the dishes on the counter so they could dry naturally.

Mom hated the Army way of doing dishes. She didn't like the way our kitchen was always lined with pots, pans, glasses, and small children waiting to dry off naturally. I hated it, too. That's because the scalding water left my hands red and wrinkly, but no doubt germ free.

Anyone who has been to boot camp certainly knows how to make beds, polish brass, and clean bathrooms. The only problem was that they didn't teach me how to do that stuff with three kids tugging on my pant legs and screaming for something to eat. I used to think that my time at Fort Knox was the toughest thing I'd ever gone through in my life. However, after spending three months at home washing dirty underwear and wiping runny noses, boot camp would seem like a cruise in the Bahamas.

"Pinnock, you dirt bag. Give me 50 push-ups and knock 'em out fast."

"Thank you, drill sergeant. Anything but another day with a screaming kid with a dirty diaper."

Sweet dreams, but the fact is that the Army never did call me back. My days of jumping out of airplanes and riding atop tanks were over. The Army obviously didn't drop me like a cheap grenade because of my new posting. But in my mind, it was the same thing: "Goodbye Captain Pinnock; hello Corporal Clean."

Chapter 13

Potty Training Is A Dirty Business

I t may be easier to teach a kid how to balance a checkbook than to instruct him in the use of a potty chair. There's just something about a porcelain throne and several gallons of swirling water that scares the bejabbers out of children, but bejabbers is all that they scare out of them. The kids would rather squat behind a chair and do their business in a diaper than use the toilet, even if it's a pint-sized model with pictures of Goofy on the sides.

Etched in my memory is the experience I had with Tommy and the potty chair. Logic was never involved, at least, not on Tommy's part. From my point of view, it seemed that he would have welcomed an alternative to carrying around a hefty load. Just the reduction of the noise made by the circling flies should have been welcomed. But neither the drag nor the flies nor his eye-watering bouquet ever appeared to trouble him in the least. When he saw me coming, he'd run for it, sometimes with his treasure swaying behind him in a test of gravity and my perseverance with each of his little steps.

When I'd finally snag him, it was hand-to-nose combat. Holding my breath, and wishing for a gas mask, I wrestle him into a nonsquirming posture and remove the offending garment. But no matter how hard I tried to rush the cleaning process, I could never avoid taking in air five or six times during the struggle. I'm sure that my color alternated between red and green throughout.

And it wasn't just Tommy's essence that made the operation such a horrendous task. For some inexplicable reason, he screamed and kicked all the while the change of diaper was taking place. Once the change was made, however, he would run off laughing and scampering as if the ordeal had never happened. I was rearing a Jekyll and Hyde, and considering the circumstances, I always knew when Hyde was about. It was like a terrible game for me: Hyde and go sick.

But a Tommy-load was a potential weapon, and coming to grips with one of those loads took courage. In fact, during that period, it occurred to me more than once that if the Army wanted to bring a foe to its knees quickly, all it had to do was lob in a few rounds of dirty diapers into enemy positions.

I can hear the call now: "Alpha One, we're about to be overrun by an enemy battalion. We need artillery support 1,000 meters to our direct front, over."

"Roger, Zulu Six. I copy. Your request is for artillery support in front of your position? Do you want high-explosive rounds? Over."

"Negative, Alpha One, hit 'em with the secrete weapon. Over."

"I copy. Fire dirty diapers at my command. Good luck, Zulu Six."

A minute passes on the battlefield. Then suddenly, semi-white packages full of baby do-do catapult into the sky and splatter in the midst of the advancing battalion. The sight and smell of the result is grisly and sickening, sending chills of fear down the spines of the men who have resorted to such horrible tactics.

"Alpha One, this is Zulu Six. Be advised that the enemy is retreating in hysteria. I repeat, the enemy is retreating. Lord, it's offal."

Many times, I've wondered how a child's digestive system could turn ordinary food into something that smells and looks as if it belongs in a horror movie. During my days in the trenches, I handled a few diapers that were so bad I felt guilty about putting them out with the trash. "Dispose of soiled diapers in a sanitary way,'' was a suggestion found on most disposables. They should also label them mettle detectors, because they sure tested mine.

I'm not sure what ''dispose in a sanitary way'' meant. I simply stacked them in the garbage like dangerous snowballs, but without the skull and crossbones identifying poisonous contents. Sometimes, however, I'd let the kids paint little happy faces on them, figuring it would make it easier for the garbage crews to handle. If I had one that was an especially potent number, however, I'd stuff it into an empty milk carton and sprinkle it with Old Spice.

Of course, there were those times when not even smiley faces could help. I'll never forget the day when one of Tommy's discarded diapers was so ripe with possibilities that it brought two of the trash men to their knees before they got it into the guts of the truck.

''Not enough Old Spice,'' I thought.

After that, I buried a couple of the really raunchy ones in the backyard. At the time, it seemed a harmless act. By morning, however, most of the grass over the burial site had turned brown and three gophers had hung themselves on the swing-set. When the same thing happened a few weeks later, after I buried my meat loaf, I was really insulted.

Disposable diapers are not only a stinky business, they are also a big business. On a bad day, when I had two kids in diapers at the same time, I used as many as 12 of them. At 50 cents a throw, that added up to $6 a day, $42 a week and $168 a month, but only if every month was February. Just think, the average child wears diapers for three years, so with two kids, that comes to more than $6,000 or the price of a pretty good boat. Talk about throwing money down the toilet.

After doing those calculations, I decided to get serious with my boy.

''Tommy, get your fanny in here, old buddy, old pal,'' I said. ''Today, we're going to learn how to use the potty. And if you have any hopes of me saving enough money to send you to college, you'd best be listening to Daddy. ''

Much to my surprise, he came scampering into the bathroom and actually sat down on his pint-sized potty chair. As he mounted his little throne, I tried to put him at ease by sitting on mine. So there we sat for the better part of an hour, talking about dinosaurs, Batman, lizards, and the starting lineup for the Atlanta Braves, when he finally did his business. I can't begin to tell you how excited he was about his first visible success.

"Daddy, Daddy, look what I did," he said proudly as he stood up and pointed to the bottom of his chair. "I did it all by myself."

Incredible as it might sound, I felt pretty darn good about it, too. "That's fantastic, little buddy," I said with a grin, as I reached down and gave him a kiss. "I knew you could do it. And just think, pretty soon you won't have to wear diapers any more."

"Can I keep it?" he asked in his sweetest voice.

I laughed and gave his head a gentle pat. "Well, son, it is mighty tempting, but stuff like that is meant to be flushed away," as I casually emptied his endeavor into the toilet. "It really isn't supposed to be kept around the house. Besides, we don't have anywhere to put it."

"But I want to keep it, Daddy."

"You can't, son, and that's the end of it."

As I reached for the handle, his small hand met mine. "Daddy, if you get rid of my poopy, I won't be your best friend anymore."

The tips of his tiny fingers gently rubbed my rough knuckles as his baby-blue eyes pleaded with me. I knew I had been had. Isn't it funny how the silliest things are so important to a child and later become cherished memories for the parent.

"How about if we keep it until mommy comes home?" I asked. "That way she can be real proud of you, too."

"Good idea, Daddy," he answered, giving my right leg a big hug and my knee a kiss. "You're a good Daddy, and I'm proud of you, too."

Chapter 14

It's A Boy

I'm aware that I am going on and on about this, but a lot of my peers never came to grips with my status as a homebody. Consequently, I was the victim of persistent castigation by friends, family and acquaintances, all of whom never passed up an opportunity to let me know that I was out of step. It wasn't a conspiracy exactly; it was more a bunch of individual efforts to bring a sinner back into the fold. That's probably too strong. To their way of thinking, I was like a tire out of round and they were going to do what they could to put me back into balance. The message was clear, however, either I eased back into what was considered normal behavior or I could count my past activities as my social life of the past.

For instance, one day, my best friend telephoned to tell me not to show up for the monthly poker game.

"Might upset the boys," Larry said. "You know, considering what you're doing and all. Of course, you're welcome to come over after the game and tidy up."

His words hit me with the "spear-itual" impact of a night jump into a forest from a C-130. There is no way that kind of hurt ever heals.

"No thanks, buddy," I answered, attempting unsuccessfully to keep my temper. "But I might drop by and clean your clock."

"Testy, testy," he said, maintaining the upper hand. "Come on, Tom, you know that us guys are like ancient mariners. Ladies just aren't welcome aboard."

"Very funny," I said, slamming down the receiver.

A minute later, Larry called back. "Just kidding," he said.

"I know it," I replied, relief washing over me. "Just to show you that's there's no hard feelings, I baked an apple pie today. I'll bring it over."

"Wait a minute," he said. "I told you I was kidding. There's no call for you to threaten us with your food." Then he was the one who slammed down the receiver.

"Jerk," I hissed into the dead phone, my ear ringing from the assault, then realized that something had been accomplished by me that I had only heard Karen do before. It was that hissing sound for a word that had no esses. I guess you really have to be incensed to achieve it.

In a minute or two, I calmed down, realizing that most of us guys are jerks at one time or another. Insensitive, too. That's probably why we spit and scratch and play games where we can pound one another into the ground. The excuse for all of that is testosterone. Even if we can't pronounce it, let alone spell it, the bubba in all of us senses that there is some hormone driving us to constantly test our mettle, or at the very least overcome the fears of childhood.

But with all that fighting spirit, if you will, there is one thing men could never endure even if they had the opportunity and that's having babies. No, guys, I'm not talking about the launching pad; it's the landing zone that I have in mind.

Judging from what I've seen in delivery rooms, if men had to have the babies, Webster never would have had to find a way to describe the word overpopulation. Whatever kids did come into the world would be born in areas where guys could cry, scream and moan. Then, afterwards, they would loudly compare the effect with passing a cantaloupe through a Dixie cup.

It's all speculation, of course, but I vividly remember being in the delivery room when Tommy was born. It was a bone-chilling episode that left me with a lot more respect for women everywhere.

For the most part, it's the launching pad that we guys are interested in. So you can understand that by the time I became aware that Karen and I were already in a countdown, my part in the operation was not very distinct.

It was about to get that way, however, but when Karen waltzed into the living room one afternoon, with a grin stretched from ear to ear, I didn't have a clue. I knew something was up, and the first thing that came to mind was that she had found where I had hidden the double-stuffed Oreos.

Being a working man at the time, I was allowed to sit around and do nothing. So I was lounging in my favorite chair, sipping a chocolate Yahoo and watching the Atlanta Braves. It's one of the things I did best and the one comfort I missed most after becoming a homemaker.

"Honey," my bride said, with a gleam in her eye, I've got some exciting news for you. We're going to have a baby."

Immediately, I jumped to my feet, did a little dance, gave her a high five and let out a holler. "Can you believe it!?" I shouted. "The Braves just scored another run. Were you saying something, honey?"

Her eyes took on that glacial expression that immediately made my ears block out the sound of the television.

"What?" I said, knowing for certain that I had committed some faux pas.

"Baby," she said.

"I love you, too," I said, trying to peek around her at the TV.

"No, Bozo, not me. We're going to have a baby."

This time her words hit me like a high-inside fast ball. "Are you serious?" I asked. "I mean, this isn't just one of your tricks to get me to change the channel, is it?"

As it turned out, she was very serious, and before I knew it, I couldn't do anything right. In a few days, I moved from being insensitive to being just stupid and aware that I was insensitive.

"Gosh, darling, you look beautiful today," I remember saying one fateful afternoon.

She looked at me as if I had just broken one of our wedding vows. "How can you say that?" she cried. "My dress looks like a car tarp and I need a forklift to get out of the tub."

"You're beautiful to me," I said, trying to interject a bit of calm into our conversation.

"Call me that again," she said, holding her swollen belly with both hands, "and I'll jump up and down on your head."

I can't remember how we got involved with the Lamaze method of childbirth, but I'm certain it had to do with trying to get along with a pregnant woman. The next thing you knew, I found myself in a 12-week Lamaze class with dozens of them.

In case you've been living in a cave and haven't heard about these classes, they teach women how to have babies without the use of pain-killing drugs, and to instruct men on how to behave in the delivery room without fainting or giving up their lunch.

Our classes were at a Longwood church that was right next to a Burger King. The church was a perfect place for the men. We'd sit around and pray that we wouldn't get one of those doctors who'd insist that we watch the entire delivery, and then after it was over, hold up the placenta like it was an eight-pound bass.

"It sure is a beauty," we could imagine him saying. "Would you like to touch it?"

While the men were praying, the women spent most of their time at the Burger King eating French fries and cheeseburgers.

When I told my dad I planned to stay at Karen's side during the delivery, he wrinkled up his nose, looked me hard in the eyes and swore. "That's about the dumbest thing I ever heard in my life," he said. "Men are supposed to stay in the waiting room, smoke cigars and talk about football."

"But, Dad," I argued, "things are different now. Besides, I want to see my kid come into the world."

"Listen, Son, your mom and I had a bunch of kids and I wasn't there to see one of them born. Now that I think about it, neither was your mom."

"What do you mean, Dad?"

"I mean that she was so drugged she didn't know who some of you kids were until second or third grade."

In spite of my father's warnings, I continued with the classes, and once a week, Karen and I sat atop pillows, learned how to breathe properly and looked at films of women with smiles on their faces giving natural birth. It was obvious to me at least that having a baby was going to be a piece of cake, a simile I'd never dare to use around Karen.

When the big day finally came, I was playing golf with Karen's father, Davie. I was about to head into the woods to look for my last shot, when a man drove up in a golf cart.

"Your name Tom?" he asked.

"That's me," I answered, "and I'm sorry about hitting that lady on the last hole."

"Oh, she'll be all right once she starts breathing again," he assured me. "It's your wife you'd better worry about. She just called and said she's gone into labor."

Immediately, I began hollering for Davie, who was looking for my ball in a clump of palmetto bushes. "Karen's getting ready to have the baby," I shouted.

Davie came running out. "Guess we'd better hustle if we're going to get in 18 holes," he said.

He was just kidding of course, we only had enough time for nine before rushing home. As I moved to Karen's side, she let out a tremendous squeal.

"Gosh, honey, are your contractions hurting that much?" I asked.

"No, dummy," she bellowed, "you just stepped on my foot. How many times have I told you not to wear golf shoes in the house?"

She was already hurting, and here I made her hurt worse, which caused some concern. But I got over it. "What the heck," I thought, "if her foot doesn't stop bleeding by the time we reach the hospital, we'll be at the right place to get it stitched up."

Karen and I had been excellent students during the Lamaze classes, so I figured that having the baby naturally was going to be like sinking a two-foot putt. That was before the first big contraction hit.

"Drugs," she screamed, grabbing me so that the knuckle of the forefinger on her throwing arm was pressing into my Adam's apple. "I want drugs."

With some effort, I pulled out of her grasp. "Honey, you don't need that stuff," I calmly whispered into her ear as I looked at my stop watch to time her contractions. "Remember what we learned in Lamaze class. We can do this."

"WE," she screamed again, wildly reaching for the red spot she had just put on my throat. "What's this WE stuff," Then, without provocation, she questioned the authority of the man who officiated at my parents' wedding. "Get me painkillers before I stuff that stop watch up your nose."

The next few hours were agonizing, and from what I witnessed they weren't all that easy for Karen either. After 10 hours of labor and two hours of pushing, I was exhausted. Finally, the doctor decided to perform an emergency C-section.

When baby Tommy finally made his debut, his head was battered and bruised, both eyes were swollen shut, and a purple bump bulged from his forehead. Even his tiny lips were blue and puffy. The doctor said he would be fine as he placed him into my arms. I'm not ashamed to admit it, but there were tears rolling down my cheeks as I handed Karen our son.

"Why, he looks just like you," she said to me with a wink and a smile that still warms my heart at the memory.

When I walked into the waiting room, the first person I saw was my dad. He was sitting in a chair, with his feet up on a table reading Sports Illustrated.

"It's a boy," I said with pride. "He's a little banged up, but the doc says he's going to be fine."

"That's great, Son. Now let's get some cigars and a few beers, so we can celebrate. And don't try telling me about what went on in there because I don't want to hear it."

"Not even the part about the placenta?"
"Especially that part."

Chapter 15

Going For The Gold

I t was a little after 11 one night and I'd just finished unloading the dishwasher and packing Lindsay's lunch of a Tatertot sandwich, cherry Pop Tart, and an Atomic Fire Ball for dessert.

Since my chores were done, I was practicing my putting stroke on the living room carpet. I wanted to be on top of my game since the kids and I had planned a trip to Miniature Golf World the next day as soon as Lindsay got home from school. Practice was important inasmuch as Lindsay had been humbling me lately at the windmill and the over-and-under tees. It was so frustrating to watch her pop the ball through those obstacles with one shot while I banged around looking for an opening. It wouldn't have been so bad if she hadn't been doing so well in arithmetic, too. She knew the score.

As you may know, Miniature Golf World is near Hub Cap World, which is down the street from Sea Shell World and about a block south of Flea Market World. In Central Florida, if you don't have world in your name, you belong on another planet.

I had just sunk a couple of tough putts underneath the couch, around a plant and into an empty potato chip can when I heard Karen cry out from the bedroom.

"Honey, I don't seem to have any underwear for tomorrow. Are there any clean?"

"They must be somewhere," I answered. "Let me check."

Laying my putter down, I scampered over to the clean pile of clothes stacked on the dining room table. Nothing. I, then, ran to the laundry room and searched the dryer, coming up with a couple of big lint balls, and a half-eaten Gummy Bear.

"Good grief," I said to myself, quickly going through the baskets of clean laundry I had left there waiting to be folded. "I can't believe this."

With all of the wash I had done, how in the name of Downy could I have missed doing Karen's underwear?

"Did you find any?" she called again.

"Not yet," I yelled back.

"Maybe you stuck mine in with Lindsay's by mistake," she suggested.

"No, honey," I said, "I haven't had a chance to put Lindsay's clothes away yet."

I was beginning to feel the pressure. Looking around, I spotted the basket of dirty laundry I had placed in an empty washtub so I could do them the next day. Quickly sorting through the basket, I found Karen's underwear under a stack of ripe towels.

"Found 'em," I yelled.

"Bring them in here, will you?" she called back.

"They'll be ready in the morning," I said.

"What?"

"In the morning," I yelled.

There was no choice but to wash and dry them, and that meant not finishing until after midnight. Sighing over my negligence, I adjusted the water temperature, started the machine, put in the soap and underwear and went into the living room to fetch my putter and golf ball. As long as I had to stand there until her undies were done, I figured I might as well get in some extra practice. "I'll show Lindsay a real windmill shot," I mumbled, aiming at the hole I had made in an empty soap bottle.

It seemed as if there was always something to accomplish around the house, and not just the homemaker things. There were washers to replace, screen doors to be adjusted, curtain rods to be refastened, and all the repairs that Karen accomplished by herself while I was still working at the newspaper. Those things didn't bother me as much as the regular chores, which had a way of coming loose as soon as they were accomplished. Once done, it wasn't long before they needed doing again. It didn't matter how many dirty dishes or smelly clothes I tackled in a day, or how often I vacuumed, washed the windows or scrubbed the bathroom, there were always replacements, which seemed to grow faster than the overlap on a beer drinker's belly. It was an endless cycle that ground at me with the relentless irritation of a leaky faucet. The difference was that a faucet could be fixed.

So it occurred to me in my moments of weary reflection that we need to do something to bring honor and prestige to those who do housework. I've mulled over this prospect and it popped into my mind that something big might be in the offing here. So just remember you heard it here first. Here is my idea: housework should be an Olympic event.

Oh sure, go ahead and laugh, but consider this: bringing housework into the sports world would force homemakers to sharpen their skills and fine tune their techniques. All we need is a handful of events, and I'm sure if we put our heads together, we could come up with some worthy ideas. For starters, we could have something as simple as the Diaper Dash or the Laundry Toss.

Think of the possibilities. The Diaper Dash would be on the order of a rodeo. We could lead off with a bulldogging event. All we'd need would be a big ring and a 3-year-old wearing a dirty diaper. At the sound of the bell, a competitor would leap into the ring, chase down the toddler, pin the child to the canvas, and change its diaper. It would be a time and emotion event, in which the competitors would earn extra points for style and keeping their lunch intact. If a soiled diaper got kicked into the seats, an alert fan could take it home as a souvenir.

I can hear it now: "Golly, Tom, what's that lumpy semi-white thing on the mantel?"

"Oh, that's the dirty diaper I nabbed on the fly at the Olympic Games. If you look closely, you can see where I had the contestant sign the thing right on the soiled spot."

"That's disgusting," they'd say in disbelief. "That thing could make a buzzard gag."

"Yeah, isn't it great? I was lucky. Had to fight a couple of old women and a little kid to get it. It was worth it in spite of the fact that the one little lady pinched me on the soft part under my arm. And she did it just as I reached out to keep it from beaning her."

"You've got to be kidding."

"Gospel," I answer. "She had blue hair and was wearing an Acapulco Hard Rock Cafe T-shirt."

"Now, I know you're kidding."

"Gospel," I repeat. "No bra either."

The other game, Laundry Toss, could use the same ring. Instead of toddlers, we'd need a pile of dirty clothes, a washing machine, and a dryer. At the sound of the bell, contestants would sort the clothes and then loft them into the washing machine from a distance of 10 feet.

When the wash was complete, the athletes would then load the wet clothes into the dryer, and put another load into the washer. Once dry, the clothes would be folded and put away. Points would be deducted for lost socks, wrong temperature settings, and too much static. Any player causing colors to run would be taken outside and flogged with men's dirty underwear.

I know you think this is an imaginary nonsense, but at least consider it. Homemakers are probably some of the best athletes in the world. They have quick hands, splendid hand-to-eye coordination and can bend and scoop up a wriggling child on the run faster than a Major Leaguer can field a grounder and toss it to first base.

It doesn't take a superstar to throw a block into a 260-pound tackle. After all, football linemen are as big as pickup trucks and as slow as repairmen. But try to block a one-year-old on a crawl out of a crib.

You want to see fast? Fast is a mother trying to get her toddler to the bathroom on time. Lighting fast is the same mother getting the kid there when she doesn't have a change of underwear handy.

Homemakers are unsung heroes who need people to look up to them just like in other professions. Indeed, we need to recognize these bigger-than-life athletes worthy of emulating, the superstars who can cook tasty meals, balance a checkbook, and entertain a houseful of children all at the same time.

Getting back to the games: We could come up with a team concept? For instance, we could take a house, expose it to a bunch of kids for a couple of hours, and then send in a team of five highly skilled homemakers. Their efforts would be time-scored on their ability to white-glove clean the house from top to bottom, from the kitchen to the bathroom.

This is the sort of sport we need at the high school and college level, especially for us guys. In the Army, I used to wonder why we bothered to teach recruits the art of foxhole digging. Any fool knows that once the shooting starts, a spade in the hands of an infantryman is going to move into the ground under his feet faster than a backhoe through sand.

Innate skills, however, do not come into play regarding housework. Even under fire, there is no natural response such as digging a foxhole. These skills are learned, honed and motivated by expediency and necessity.

So in school, we are taught the basic art of individual and team sports, which is good as far as it goes. Obviously, most of us keep on running the rest of our lives, going through hoops, avoiding pitfalls and trying to keep our heads above water. But, somehow, when we put down the baseball bats, basketballs and football helmets, we have to be reminded about being a team player, especially in the home.

Consider where we might be today if we had been coached in the cleaning of baseboards and the stripping of beds — abilities to last a lifetime. If we had and used them, our wives would be so grateful that they'd probably let us watch an occasional football game without the uncontrollable urge to snipe.

At-home teamwork would get so big that we would form a Professional Homemakers' Tour (PHT). The PHT — a sure winner with such sponsors as Tide, Pampers and Betty Crocker — could offer top money and prizes. Such steps would go a long way in giving homemakers the attention and respect they deserve.

The PHT might even attract top-notch athletes from other sports. Can you imagine speed skater Bonnie Blair sweeping through a house, mopping floors and dunking dirty clothes into a laundry basket? Now that I think of it, Chris Everett might be the perfect athlete to get the PHT off the ground. Why just look at what she did for women's tennis. Now that she's retired from the court and has a family of her own, she'd be terrific.

Just the thought of a professional such as Everett baking pies, cleaning tubs and washing windows perks me up. I've seen her do tennis videos on how to improve your backhand. Perhaps, she could do one on how to serve up the perfect six-minute supper, or how to keep in shape by doing aerobics to the Bunny Hop.

Yep, with a bit of work, and by recruiting the right people, in no time we could have the PHT right up there with the NFL. Or maybe even with "This Old House."

Chapter 16

Dishing It Out

T o this day, I wake up in the middle of the night wondering if I've packed Lindsay's lunch, if there was enough milk for breakfast, if I've put the clothes in the dryer, if I've fed the dog, and if I turned in the money for the school fund-raiser. When I realize it's just a ghastly nightmare, I say a quick prayer and go back to sleep. I think I'd rather have a root canal on the back of a two-hump camel than go through that again.

I've done a lot of wacky things in my life — I once grabbed a 10-foot alligator by the tail because I thought it was dead — but I think my addlebrained bet with Karen topped them all. When the countdown to winning my bet was at 30 days, which is a million peanutbutter sandwiches in homemaker lingo, I realized I had a better chance of becoming a gourmet cook in that time. An even more remote possibility was that I had more of an opportunity to match up all the socks in the laundry room than sticking it out for the remaining 720 hours. As much as I wanted that graphite golf club, I wanted out from under the weight of my apron even more.

After only two months on the home front, I saw signs that made me wonder if my apron was on a little too tight. It had gotten to the point where I started making up names for the familiar towels, shirts, pants and other things that I had to keep picking up around the house. I even had names for some of the dishes, silverware, and glasses.

A few, I even grew quite fond of. Take, for example, my brown coffee mug Dumbo, which was decorated with white African elephants. Actually, I started with four elephant mugs, then there was only one, and even that one was a bit battered. Perhaps, I was partial to Dumbo because of what happened to the other three mugs.

It was an innocent act of playfulness that cost the pachyderm cups their existence. For a Christmas present, Aunt Linda and Uncle Joe had given Tommy a small Noah's Ark — less than a cubit long. The toy came with a herd of colorful animals that, two by two, began to disappear.

By May, there remained only one rhinoceros, two giraffes and a headless hippopotamus. Tommy especially missed the elephants, and one morning when he saw me drying off three of the pachyderm mugs, he asked if he could use them in his little yellow ark.

"Of course you can, little buddy," I said. "Just be careful with them."

"You're sharing aren't you, Daddy? You're a good boy for sharing."

Filling with pride over a lesson learned by my small son, I didn't think much more about the mugs until a short time later when I spotted Tommy on the patio tossing his ark at a lizard.

"What are you doing, little fella?" I asked as the ark bounced off the screen, slid across the top of Tommy's playhouse and crashed onto the concrete.

"I'm catching lizards to put in my ark, Daddy."

"That's great, son, but what did you do with the elephants that I gave you?"

"What elephants, Daddy?"

"You know, the ones that were on daddy's favorite coffee mugs."

"Those weren't very good elephants, Daddy."

Somehow, I knew what was coming next, so I wasn't surprised when I found what was left of the pachyderm cups in a zillion pieces at the bottom of the ark along with one very frightened lizard.

Of course, that little incident was nothing compared to the one involving our dishes. In my defense, let me just say that if we hadn't run out of paper plates and cups when we did, the whole mess could have been avoided. As it turned out, we were destined to use a lot more paperware than we ever had before.

It all began one rainy day as I prepared lunch for Tommy and Ashley. That's when I discovered we were out of paper plates and cups. It may sound tacky, but I hated using real glasses and ceramic plates, because it meant having to wash them. That is, unless I could get the kids to lick them clean which, with my cooking, was out of the question. My options gone, I was forced to bring out the ceramic ware and, of course, the children messed that up in no time at all.

Watching them eat took a strong stomach, so most of the time, I looked away. Since we were working with breakable stuff, however, I felt compelled to monitor what they were doing.

I did OK until they smeared their lightly toasted peanut butter and banana sandwiches into their buttered grits and then smushed it all into their plates, bowls and even a Bugs Bunny mug. Just the effort involved in producing this mess made my stomach flip-flop. When they actually ate it, I could feel the green washing over me.

After that ordeal was over, everything had to be washed and put away. But as luck would have it, when I went to the sink to rinse off the scummy dishes, I discovered that some knucklehead had turned off the water. I didn't know if it was because I had forgotten to pay the water bill or if the city had just shut the system down for a time and I hadn't remembered the notice.

In any case, I didn't want dirty dishes sitting in the sink all day. By now, you know that I am not a neat freak, neither am I afraid of my little wife. In spite of that, I have no desire to flip on her mouth engine either.

Most of the time Karen is sweet and soft-spoken, but when provoked, she can get a choke hold on me and let loose with her opinions until my ears ring. So I didn't want her arriving home from work, spotting traces of lunch on the plates, and getting a lecture. The last one sapped my strength for an hour after she let loose.

"At McDonalds, they get happy meals," she said, the whites around the blue in her eyes, growing redder by the second. "I try to give them healthy meals, and you feed them goofy meals, Bozo." (That's one of her pet names for me). Then, ignoring my protests, she tossed the kids supper into the garbage.

"What are doing?" I asked in disbelief. "There's nothing wrong with that food."

"Nothing wrong!" she said as if softness had never been part of her speech pattern. Then, as she pointed one forefinger at the garbage can, she began wagging the other at me. "You were going to feed my babies Ding-Dongs and pork rinds for supper. Are you beginning to walk with one foot off the curb? Did you hear too many big booms when you were in the Army?"

I was beginning to see her point. Ding-Dongs and pork rinds are more of a lunch combination than a main meal, but I was surprised that she knew about my walking habits.

"Now, wait a minute," I said, stalling for time. When my mind drew a blank, I just stood there and accepted the tongue-lashing.

During my years in the Army, I heard some tough drill sergeants, but their speech techniques were wimpy compared to that of my bride on the warpath. The sergeants' language was stronger, but it had none of Karen's incisive cerebral melt. In five minutes, she could challenge my IQ, and then reduce the measurement by 25 points.

To prevent permanent damage to my self-respect, I began retreating faster than an Iraqi tank company during the Gulf War, knowing full well that I was fortunate to escape without acquiring a permanent hundred-yard stare. I had learned my lesson, and after that, I never gave the children Ding-Dongs and pork rinds again, not even when she wasn't around.

Looking back, I have examined Karen's objections to my menu selection, over and again. When I finally figured it out, I could better understand her anger. Pork rinds go much better with corn chips. Ding-Dongs are a dessert.

It was to avoid another brain check that I wanted to wash away the residue of something she didn't approve of on one of the kids' plates. With that in mind, I carted the dirty dishes out into the yard, only to find that it was no longer raining, at least not enough to get rid of any signs of lunch.

For a minute, frustration flooded over me. Then I spotted the water still coming off the roof of the garage. Figuring that would probably be enough to do the trick, I scattered the cups, glasses and dishes under the biggest drips in the driveway. After that, I returned to the house to finish my chores.

When I did my scattering, it seemed a brilliant way to resolve my worry. The problem was that I forgot about what I had done until it was time for me to pick up Lindsay at school. As I was backing the car out of the garage, my memory returned in a flash. It happened as soon as I heard the sound of plates shattering under the car.

"What was that, Daddy" Tommy asked as bits of glass shot past his window.

Immediately, I could visualize what I had done. There was no point in even examining the damage.

"Dishes, Son," I replied to Tommy. "I just crushed all our dishes."

"Mommy isn't going to like that," he said, a warning in his small voice.

"You're right, little buddy," I answered with more cheerfulness than I felt. "But, at least, Mommy can't fuss at us for leaving them in the sink."

Later, when we returned with Lindsay, I swept up the shattered mess. "I'll be darned," I said to no one, "they did get pretty clean after all."

That's when I noticed the remains of a brown elephant mug.

"They're extinct now," I thought. "Just like I'm going to be when Karen gets home."

Chapter 17

Grocery Store Blues

I've never cared much for grocery shopping and, when I was doing it once a week, I hated it. Partly, it was because women gave me funny looks when I was fumbling through my bag of coupons at the cash register. Mostly, it was because they never even bothered to whisper when they made their comments about me. It was as if I were deaf or an idiot.

For instance, one gray-haired grande dame in a flowered halter nodded at me then said to the cashier in a New England accent, "Looks like the President's work program for the mentally challenged is stumbling."

Another referred to me as Tom Thumbs. After that I stopped wearing the T-shirt with my name on it.

It wasn't that they weren't using coupons as well, but they had been at it longer, and were better organized. I sympathized with them for having to wait for me while I sorted through the stack, but their comments often hit below the belt. What would you think if you heard a grandmother say, "I bet he'd fail a stool test, too." That was her assessment after I asked the woman with her about the difference between a baking potato and a red potato.

However, those remarks were mild compared to the brutal things they said if one of my kids happened to flip a half-eaten Ding-Dong into their cart. I remember one particularly graphic utterance by an attractive young woman in jeans and a Key West "Save the Bales" sweatshirt. The bales on her shirt referred to a practice by dope smugglers of dumping marijuana into the Atlantic if the DEA closed in on them. As she wheeled off in a huff, an older man pulled his cart up to mine, grinned and said, "Do you think she eats with that mouth?"

Still stunned by what she said and by her parting gesture, I just shrugged and tried to smile. "I don't think I've ever seen three rings on one finger before."

"Don't worry," he said, "you'll catch on. They can tell you're a greenhorn at this and just want to intimidate you."

"How do they know?" I asked.

"You look bewildered," he responded.

All of this used to embarrass me so much that I wouldn't go to the same store twice in a row, which was a mistake, because you have to learn the layout.

One of the keys to successful shopping is store familiarization. Most men have trouble finding their way around grocery stores to begin with, but when it's one they have never been in before, well, they're likely to get lost for days. I know, because I was one of the wanderers. Fellows in that situation are easy to spot. They're the ones bumping about the aisles like blind dogs looking for a fireplug.

After a few solo trips, I started taking Lindsay to the supermarket with me, realizing that most girls have a lot of mom in them. Almost instinctively, they develop shopping tricks such as what people should eat, and how much, where the stuff is found and the kind of packaging it comes in.

At a grocery store, those miniatures of their moms are generally more capable than men. Maybe it's in the chromosomes — the XX vs. the XY thing that determines the boy thing and the girl thing — or maybe the comic who pointed out that men are hunters and women gatherers is right, because if chicken was at the top of my shopping list, I'd head for the meat counter, ignoring everything else along the way.

Lindsay accompanied me, her eyes, like Karen's, moving back and forth in a search-light pattern. By the time I found my prey, a dead chicken in this particular case, she gathered 10 things that we needed: milk, cheese, juice, apples, eggs, biscuits, lettuce, tomatoes, carrots, potatoes and bread.

To keep from embarrassing myself, I never let on that I had not even seen most of what she had picked up, even though we had passed all of them along the way.

I may not have been an "A" student in the President's mentally challenged program, but I could spot a natural team when I saw one: one hunter, one gatherer.

So men, if you find it necessary to go to the supermarket to hunt for food and you have a little gatherer in the house, take her along. Your time there will be a much more pleasant experience, and probably a lot less time-consuming, too.

For starters, little girls make excellent scouts and retrievers. Here's how it works. As you're pushing the cart along, and you're actually thinking and not just stalking a dead chicken, send her ahead to locate items you know won't be easy to find, such things as stewed Italian tomatoes or ripe zucchini. While she's busy searching out the toughies, you can plod along and grab the easy stuff like bread, milk, and eggs..

And when your runner returns, don't hesitate to send her out on another mission. Have her fetch the bottle liners, formula, baby diapers and sanitary napkins. Oh sure, you'll eventually find them, but once you do, you won't be able to remember what kind of formula to get, what size diapers to buy and your mind will go blank on that last item. There are just too many to choose from, and the more you look, the more confused you become. But little girls will know about every one of those items, even the last one. And if you forget that last one, you'll have to come back with a note to fetch it by yourself. It's a punishment wives use on their husbands to improve their memories and test their staying power.

So the father-small daughter team is a beautiful system, especially once your scout is thoroughly trained and properly motivated. Once the teamwork thing is worked out, you can hang out around the lobster tank or the magazine rack and drink coffee while she does all the hard stuff. And don't feel guilty about it either. Instead, take it for what it is: on-the-job, future-mom training.

As for motivation, it's essential to properly reward your gatherer for her efforts. If you don't, she might balk the next time you try to recruit her help. The reward system is as vast as your imagination. Some dads simply allow their gatherers to pick out their favorite snacks as they shop. Others take their girls to the movies, or buy them toys once the shopping trip is complete.

But with Lindsay it was different. She enjoys my company and she really couldn't care less about a box of cookies or a day at the movies. All I had to do was promise to buy her a car when she turns 16.

Here's another little trick that will make your shopping more productive. Let's say you're supposed to bring home a couple of steaks, two pounds of hamburger and a chicken worthy of baking. Don't just pluck something out of the cooler that you think might work. I once picked out meat that was so tough my dog couldn't gnaw through it.

To keep from making expensive mistakes pick out a woman examining the selections in the meat case. Approach her with a sad and helpless look on your face, and say in your most pathetic voice, ''Sorry to bother you, Ma'am, but my wife was run over by a cement truck last week, and I was wondering if you might be kind enough to help me pick out a roast, and a steak, and maybe a turkey for my little girl here?''

The first time I tried this a woman took three steps backwards and threw both hands over her face. I figured I'd really gotten to her before I remembered that I had had garlic pickles with lunch.

''Sorry,'' I said.

''Rosenblum's Deli?'' she said.

I nodded and tried to keep a safe distance. In spite of my offending air, she made a number of terrific suggestions, even giving me a hint regarding the pot roast she had picked out. I didn't develop into a gourmet cook, but everything I made after that stayed down.

This little drill worked so well that I have removed the gamble in shopping for meat. But in any ploy, you have to use caution. I once made a woman feel so bad about my circumstances that she not only did all my shopping, but she wanted to pay for my groceries, too. If she had had enough food stamps, I might have let her.

Another time, a kindly grandmother wanted to come home and fix supper for us. While I was considering it, she mentioned that she had a recently widowed daughter.

"Emma Mae lost her husband to a runaway dump truck just last month," she said.

"Wow, what a coincidence," I said.

"You'd make such a sweet couple," she said as she shuffled through some ground round. "And you certainly wouldn't have to worry about your ex's bothering you."

"Wow, what a coincidence," I repeated stupidly, then turned and got the heck out of there.

If you're in a hurry, there's yet another way to get your shopping done. Simply stroll about the store until you spot a cart that has a lot of the same things in it that you like. Wait for the person filling the cart to meander away, then grab the cart and bolt for the checkout counter. This, however, is not a good practice when children are with you. Their short legs will slow you down too much.

As I've pointed out, Lindsay was always a blessing in the store, but my son was a different story. Tommy tried to eat his way through the aisles. What he didn't eat, he wanted to toss into the cart.

"Son, would you mind putting that turkey back in the freezer, and please take those marshmallows out of your mouth."

"But they taste good, Daddy."

"How can they taste good? You haven't even taken them out of the bag. Now forget about them and help me pick out some cereal. What kind do you want?"

"That one and that one and that one and that one..."

"We can't get them all."

"Why not?" he asked, a hurt expression on his little face.

"Because we have to get some other food, too."

"Why?"

"Because not even daddy serves cereal for every meal."

"Why?"

"Because cereal is supposed to be for breakfast. Besides, it's up to me to feed you right so when you grow up, you can be big and strong and play inside linebacker for the Miami Dolphins. Not only that, but your mommy would kill me if she knew that I was feeding you cereal three times a day. Now, what do you want me to get for supper?"

"How about coffee cake, Daddy? I like that!"

"Great. Let's see if we can find the coffee cake aisle."

Before I stayed home with the kids, I had no idea what a tough job it was to get children to eat properly, or, for that matter, to get them to eat at all. One day, they love scrambled eggs and the next, they hate them. For two straight weeks, they ate nothing but Magilla Gorilla Burgers, and then suddenly they turned on them like they were diseased and rotten. Fortunately, I came up with my own way to deal with my fussy little crumb snatchers.

Breakfast — This was always a difficult time because Karen was getting ready for work, Lindsay was getting dressed for school and Tommy was looking for cartoons on the TV. Ashley spent her time underneath my feet trashing the cabinets...smash, crash, whaaaa. If at all possible, try and avoid this chaotic time by staying in bed.

If your wife insists that you get up, go into the bathroom and lock the door. With any luck, she will give up on you, knowing that once you're in there, you probably won't see you for days. Then, maybe she'll go ahead and dress the kids, pack lunches, and fix breakfast. If she doesn't, and sometimes wives can be stubborn about these things, you have no choice but to meander into the thick of things.

Once you've made your move to face the screaming horde, however, never, I repeat, never, attempt to make breakfast. Instead, try doing something less stressful — fetch the paper, check the weather channel, walk the dog or practice your golf swing. The fact is that mornings are not suitable for preparing food, especially when the mom of the house is looking over your shoulder to see if you are making something nutritionally sound.

Instead, wait until she leaves for work before feeding the children. That way you can serve up last night's spaghetti or leftover pizza. If that doesn't work, try cake or popcorn. Kids love stuff like that, and it's a lot easier than making pancakes or waffles.

Lunch — Lunch was not nearly as difficult as breakfast because Karen was at work, which meant that the pressure was off. I found that I could almost always get the children to eat ice cream sodas for their noon meal. Merely plop a couple of scoops of vanilla or chocolate ice cream into a paper cup and pour in some root beer. Presto, you have a fun meal. Don't forget to destroy all evidence of this meal by throwing away the paper cup.

Dinner — This was the most difficult of all meals to serve. There were a number of reasons for this: I was exhausted from housework, the kids were tired and fussy, and I knew that Karen would be home at any moment. If my timing was off, I feared that she might catch me feeding the little ones Mickey Mouse popsicles for supper. I got over this fear by loading them into the car and taking them to McDonalds, Taco Bell or Hot-dog World. It was safer that way.

Chapter 18

The Day No Kids Would Cry

I 'll be the first to admit that I was a flop as a househusband. My cooking would have made Betty Crocker weep. And cleaning? Well, the dirty laundry grew so high that the Federal Aviation Administration made me put a blinking red light on top of it. You know that's an exaggeration; the Feds never got involved. It was the county that stepped in.

To make matters worse, I really didn't fit in with the neighborhood housewives. Not once was I invited to a Tupperware party. No one ever knocked on my door to borrow an egg or ask for a recipe. Even our good friend and neighbor, Jan, remarked one day that the only thing that matched the quality of my cooking and cleaning was my fishing.

"That hurts," I said. "What's wrong with this place?"

Since we were standing in the kitchen, my timing for that particular question was really stupid. She looked at me, then at the sink. My eyes followed hers as she examined the unwashed dishes, the curtain that had half slipped from the rod hanging over the main window, and the foul-smelling mop leaning over a pail of dirty water that reeked of Tommy after a trip to the mall.

"Want a list?" she asked.

"What do you mean, a list?" I demanded half-heartedly, knowing, of course, that the place was not up to snuff.

"Certainly, there must be something that you can do well, Tom."

"Sure there is," I said, thinking of the children. It may sound corny, but I did do well with the kids. They missed Karen, of course, and on some mornings, they even cried when she hustled off to work. But most of the time, the kids and I weren't living a Greek tragedy. We were having fun together. I appreciated being around them, and I know they loved having me home.

In fact, I still cherish the days we spent at the playgrounds chasing after pigeons and spinning on the merry-go-rounds. Also, once I got over my self-consciousness about pushing a stroller, my morning walks with Ashley reached No. 1 on my hit list. It was then, when my inhibitions were at their lowest, that I could bellow out a few choruses of "The Hokey Pokey" or the "The Bunny Hop" as we moved along. I know she loved it, too, because to this day, she refers to me as her best buddy.

After being around the children for three months, I knew I would find a way of spending as much time with them as possible. As it turned out, not only did I get to stay home, but so did my beautiful bride. We had no way of knowing it then, but because of that small business that I had alluded to earlier, within five years, our income would exceed a million dollars and we would be living in a beautiful home on a golf course outside of St. Louis.

We also became partners in fixing dinner, making sure the children had on clean underwear and assaulting the laundry mountain, which, once reduced, never rose again.

The freedom we had sought, as well as that ever-elusive bit of sanity, were about to become ours. It would take a while yet before it really struck in a big way, but I was determined to make it work. Because in the 90 days that I had been developing housemaid's knee, I knew I didn't ever want to do it full-time again, and I didn't want that for Karen either. From that point on, it was to be a shared experience.

You probably want to know if I got the golf club that Karen promised me if I stuck it out the entire three months. No, I didn't. However, I didn't have to do dishes solo either. So it turned out to be a draw. I didn't get the golf club because the agreement was that I had to fly solo for 90 days, and I didn't quite make it. The dishes were a different thing. Once we moved to Atlanta, our business grew so fast that we made enough money for us to invest in a top-notch dishwasher.

By the time Karen rejoined the household as a full-time mom, my hands were cracked and red from washing dishes and scrubbing floors. I'd gotten scrub-brush elbow and was afraid there was little hope that I'd ever be able to correctly grip a tennis racquet or a golf club again.

I knew I wouldn't be invited back to play on the tennis team. Nor were my old cronies going to count me in their foursomes on the golf course. The boys were obviously embarrassed about what I had been doing and let if be known that after three months of kneeling and wheeling, the chances of my breaking 100 on the links did not seem part of my near future. At least, not in their company. Not that it really mattered. A short time later, we headed for Georgia.

You have to take the bad with the good. The good occurred on the afternoon I informed the children that Karen was going to quit her job to be at home, too. I wanted to tell them all at one time, but the house was such a mess I couldn't find Ashley. For a moment, I was in a panic, then something familiar wafted by. The comic is right, those disposable diapers just won't hold the advertised load.

As I was changing her, I related the news. The children reacted immediately, and with great enthusiasm. "Hip, hip, hooray," Lindsay and Tommy screamed, tossing pillows about the room and leaping into the air.

I felt elated, too, until they began demeaning my culinary efforts.

"No more burnt cheese sandwiches," Lindsay cheered.

"No more boiled Spam," Tommy chimed in.

"Hip, hip, hooray," they chorused.

"No more helping Dad clean the house," Lindsay called out, taking over in a solo effort. "Hip, hip, hooray. No more..."

"I get the message," I said, looking around for a place to deposit the dirty diaper. My first day on the job, I learned that the redolence from one of those packed things would match a open sewer if left untended. If left for a day, the house would have had to be condemned.

Turning my attention to the cheering crowd, I told them, "Mom's coming home to stay, but we have to make it nice for her. You have plenty of time to vacuum the carpet..."

Lindsay was already ahead of me, "Yes, Dad, and paint the kitchen before we change the oil in the car."

"Right," I said, thinking that I was going to have to change my act. "I hope you studied the owner's manual like I told you. It's a darn good thing that Mom's going to be around, because it's obvious that you kids aren't doing your part. She'll put some starch into you."

"Lecture, lecture," the kids chorused, including Ashley. It was just then that Karen walked into the room. Discarding their taunt, all three rushed over and gave her big grin.

Giving each of the children a quick kiss and a hug, she asked, "How's everyone doing today?"

It was Tommy who cried out. "Daddy's been a bad boy."

I was stunned. "How can you say that?" I asked in dismay. "Didn't I take you to the grocery, the dry cleaners and the gas station today?"

"I wanted a toy," Tommy said, looking to his mother for support.

"A toy!" I exclaimed. "Why that's just what we need around here is another toy. We have toys in the garage, in your bedroom, on the patio, in the attic, behind the chairs in the living room and in every closet in the house."

"Lecture, lecture," Lindsay and Tommy chorused.

But they weren't going to intimidate me. I stuck to my guns, saying, "I've spent the last three months picking up your dinosaurs, your G.I. Joes, your trains, your trucks, your stuffed animals and enough building blocks to construct homes for half of the homeless people in North America."

"Lecture, lecture," they all chimed in, including Karen and Ashley.

I was hurt, I was stern, I was angry, I was sorry I had forgotten about the squirt gun that Tommy had wanted, because right then, I would have nailed them all.

So what did I do? You bet, I kept right on lecturing, saying "I throw oodles of toys away each week, and not once have you asked me about anything missing. You didn't even say anything about the toy lawn mower, the one that blew bubbles and made more noise than a chainsaw."

When I said that, it was as if I had struck him. Immediately, his grin was replaced by tears. He wailed, "Mommy, he threw out my favorite toy. I told you he was being bad."

"Don't worry about it, honey," Karen answered, patting his head and giving me a pretend dirty look. "Mommy will watch Daddy from now on."

My lecture wasted, there was nothing to do but smile. It was a smile that had been growing in me ever since that morning when Karen and I decided that this would be her last day on the job.

My heart was doing cartwheels. As I regarded my family and saw their happiness, I knew that this was the day that no kids would cry, at least after Tommy got finished. Mom was going to be home and so was I, and all because of that little business that I had started working off our kitchen table.

But what happened on our march to those millions is another story.